2008

With best wishes
Enjoy

Ruan Vernon

Doug Spence

WEST POINT MARKET
Cookbook

Series on Ohio History and Culture

WEST POINT MARKET
Cookbook

RUSS VERNON

Foreword by David Giffels, Illustrations by Doug Spence

THE UNIVERSITY OF AKRON PRESS • AKRON, OHIO

All rights reserved • First Edition 2008 • Manufactured in the United States of
America • All inquiries and permission requests should be addressed to the Pub-
lisher, The University of Akron Press, Akron, Ohio 44325-1703.

12   11   10   09   08   5   4   3   2

LIBRARY OF CONGRESS CATALOGING-IN-PUBLICATION DATA

Vernon, Russ, 1938–

West Point Market cookbook / by Russ Vernon ; foreword by David Giffels ;
illustrations by Doug Spence. — 1st ed.

p. cm. — (Series on Ohio history and culture)

Includes index.

ISBN 978-1-931968-58-4 (cloth : alk. paper)

1. Cookery.   2. West Point Market.   I. West Point Market.   II. Title.

TX714.V457 2008

641.5—dc22

2008026518

The paper used in this publication meets the minimum requirements of American
National Standard for Information Sciences—Permanence of Paper for Printed
Library Materials, ANSI z39.48–1984. ∞

Cover image: Illustration by Doug Spence.

Contents

Foreword
The Secret Need for Octopus

I suppose it's strange to be thinking of a grocery store in terms of one's "hopes" and "dreams" and "spiritual well-being." Then again, it's strange to be thinking of West Point Market as a "grocery store."

So maybe that's why, when I think of West Point, I begin to think of wishbones. I have this unusual regard for wishbones and the entire wishbone ceremony. All my adult life, every time I have grasped that offered prong, I have affected a decidedly competitive stance, concentrated very hard, and I have always made the same wish, for This One Thing. The person on the other prong has never known this wish because the nature of wishes is that they are held inside, like suppressed hiccups, which, if no one ever told you, are actually vaporous leprechauns trying to escape through your esophagus, and the more of them you hold inside, the more likely you are to discover gold. Which is to say that my heart reserves a small place for fate and superstition.

So, after many, many years of trying, all of a sudden and with uncommon dramatic flair, This One Thing came true. It happened. I got a phone call announcing that it was for real, one of those phone calls that feels kind of like a Busby Berkeley routine, with cascading daisies forming kaleidoscopic spirals across the ceiling and the person on the other end delivering the details of This One Thing while dressed in a white tuxedo and top hat and actually singing these details in the form of a cabaret sea chanty and you, the receiver of the news, running up the wall to launch into a deft backflip that lands you in the outstretched arms of a dozen German barmaids. That sort of thing.

And my very first thought was to celebrate, to spontaneously whip up some sort of ceremony so that my wife and I could savor this moment properly, knowing that thousands of wishbones had been sacrificed in the making of this evening, and such an event was unlikely to happen again any time soon. And the first practical consideration amid the last fading notes of the Good News Concertina was that West Point Market would be closing in less than half an hour and I needed to get there pronto to select something bubbly from the wine racks and something celebratory from the Prepared Foods case; I needed to get to that place which exists for just such a moment as this.

I have never thought of West Point Market in any other way, nor should I, nor should you. In fact, as I considered how to introduce this book of West

Point recipes, my initial plan was to document a visit there to buy a bottle of ketchup. Right? You, the reader of this book, would immediately be in on the joke. No one goes to West Point Market for ketchup. You go there for other reasons entirely, reasons that only begin with food/drink and quickly rise to things of the ether and of the spirit. Dreamy things. Hopeful things. The sorts of things you hear in music and see in sunsets and that bounce around on the mattress with suppressed leprechauns.

Breathless, I jumped into the car and rushed to beat the market's closing. Naturally I wanted to share the news, and naturally, this being That Sort of Day, as I passed through the automatic glass doors I saw, standing right there at the checkout, two friends of the very sort who would want to know of this development.

These friends, whose sudden appearance is filed here under the heading "Nonfiction Suspension of Disbelief: No, Really I Am Not Making Any of This Up," were two young ladies of a certain bohemian type. The type that might, say, have spent the previous night drinking absinthe, slept through the day, and gone out to West Point Market for comfort food. (For the record, the number of friends I have in this category is statistically insignificant.) And there they were, standing right in front of me, as though this were a game of Good News pitch-and-catch.

I motioned for them to "c'mere-I-have-something-to-tell-you" and as they came closer, I detected a distinct gray cloud of what-the-cat-drug-in.

"What—" I open-ended the question.

"We drank absinthe last night."

"A bottle."

"She threw up."

I glanced toward the wine department.

"Um, you didn't. . . ."

There is no other place in all of Ohio that might prompt me toward the conclusion that this was actually where the scandalously exotic elixir had been purchased. And, no, they confirmed that the bottle had been smuggled into the country somehow, all very mysterious, and that its consumption and the aftermath represented an entire saga, the conclusion of which was that such an event could only end with cheese.

The one girl held up the bag to illustrate this.

"Guess what," I said, and I told them the news and they expressed their shared delight, although the one looked like she really could use that cheese. We said our goodbyes and I hurried then into the warm path of this place that always smells like coffee and chocolate. Allowing myself the delusion that I really could tell one bottle of Prosecco from another, I looked over the options and selected one in the middle, then hurried through the aisles to complete my mission.

There is something about this course through the store—through the Great Wine Forest, around the Whispering Cave of the Cheeses, past Mrs. Ticklemore's Tearoom (Nonfiction Suspension of Disbelief II: that's the actual name) and into the Plain of the Killer Brownies—that is at once directly familiar and just beyond objective description. Like the sound of an approaching blimp and the concept of the Don Drumm wedding gift, it's something we natives share and understand intrinsically and it improves our lives in a particularly local way. It's the best kind of provincialism, the aspect of life in a place that enjoys certain flavors exclusively. I suspect I'm like most people in these parts in that I am not a regular at West Point. I only go there when I need something special, or I want to feel in some way special. This is the place where, the only time in my life I ever needed to purchase octopus, I was able to. I bought octopus off the rack, as they say in the sport-coat business.

There is a comfort to this, the knowledge that something you didn't know you needed is available, and the knowledge that the place where you live—the deliciously mundane Akron, Ohio—is a place where other people secretly need octopus, secretly drink absinthe and occasionally, maybe once in a lifetime, have everything go dreamily right, if only for an hour or two.

And so it was on to the glass case, where I selected two breaded chicken breasts and some fancy green beans and some artichoke salad, making it to the finish line just as the lights began to click off behind me, darkening the shop to allow (presumably) the elves to creep in and do their work undetected.

Back home, we opened the Prosecco and poured, raised our glasses to toast, dimmed the chandelier, lit candles and sat down to eat. I bit into my chicken breast and when I did, my teeth connected with something. I reached up and pulled it out:

The winning end of a wishbone.

I keep it and the Prosecco cork in a little cup on my desk, as reminders of one very fine day and also as reminders that these days are rare indeed and life is so tarnished by compromise, trifle, and hurt that you need to do everything you can to keep the special places special.

I can never untangle those reminders from their source at West Point Market, nor from the recognition that the Akron landmark has been so very carefully groomed by three generations of the Vernon family that it can only be seen as a special place, one that harbors flavor and graciousness and the sorts of surprises you didn't know were coming.

—*David Giffels*

Preface

I grew up in a house where good food was always available. Not always complicated or exotic, but well-prepared. My mother was a talented lady. She sewed clothes for my two sisters, prepared dinner for the church, and made sure we had a good meal when we sat down at the table together every night. She was a butter and cream cook. Growing up with that background made me hooked on quality ingredients.

Even when I served in the Air Force in Albuquerque, New Mexico, that passion for quality continued. The PX provided our staples, but our meats and fresh vegetables came from an out-of-the-way, small family meat store. As a young married couple just starting out we had a tight budget but we knew the importance of quality food and we put my paycheck on the dinner table.

Wherever we go, I am always on the lookout for new tastes, recipes, and ideas. For forty-six years I have carried a recorder in my pocket everywhere I go so that I can bring my culinary findings back to Akron. In each town or city I visit, I look in the Yellow Pages and check out the local shops to see what new products or recipes they have to offer. My wife keeps a book in the glove compartment when we are on vacation just in case I see a sign on the highway and end up spending an hour or two at a small shop, tasting and trading recipes, or finding the supplier for a product that we just have to have.

It is this passion for business and quality that has kept West Point Market going for the past seventy-one years.

I always wanted to put together a cookbook to showcase the best West Point Market offers. Encouraged by our executive chef, our kitchen staff, my son Rick, and our president, Larry Uhl, our Cookbook Committee was formed. In our test kitchen, we tasted and perfected our family recipes, improving or substituting when we could to make them user-friendly. If it was too labor-intensive, we threw it out. When you have access to the finest, freshest ingredients, you don't need complicated recipes to appreciate those ingredients. Our test chefs had access to Belgian chocolate, homemade caramel, over three hundred and fifty types and styles of cheeses, and over eight thousand ingredients used in the finest kitchens in the country. And when you are finished cooking, you can relax and enjoy the meal with one of our three thousand wine labels.

The result: A collection of recipes we think you, your family, and your friends will love.

—*Russ Vernon*

Breakfast !

THE OMELET is an art that begins as a blank canvas for your culinary imagination. Like the versatile crepe, omelets are wonderful at any time of day. Start with an envelope of fresh Grade A eggs and fill it with your creativity. Depending on your appetite, the omelet canvas can be composed of two eggs, three eggs, or, for a lighter version, three egg whites and two egg yolks. Your choices for fillings are endless—just cheese to keep it simple, a burst of colors and flavors according to the season, or even a hearty mishmash of leftovers from the fridge. Don't worry about using one of those cute two-sided pans or omelet forks. I've been using the same ten-inch sloped-sided pan and a regular fork for fifteen years and the omelet always slips easily on the plate. As with any art, it takes practice, but the best thing is that if your creation isn't recognizable, it still tastes good. Call yourself a culinary Picasso, eat it, and try again.

West Point's Classic Omelet

You can build a whole meal around an omelet—serve steamed broccoli, asparagus, or fresh fruit as side dishes, along with a toasted, split baguette and champagne, mimosas, or Conundrum, a white wine from California. Grilled onions and peppers are our favorite base for fillings. For a lighter omelet, we use water instead of milk in the egg mixture.

INGREDIENTS:

>   3 large eggs, at room temperature
>   3 tablespoons water
>   ⅛ teaspoon sea salt
>   ¼ teaspoon freshly ground pepper
>   Fresh herbs, optional
>   3 to 4 drops Tabasco, optional
>   1 tablespoon unsalted butter
>   1 tablespoon olive oil

Filling combinations are limited only by your imagination. Here are some of our favorites from which to choose.

MEATS: sausage, crisp bacon, smoked salmon, diced cooked chicken breast, ground sirloin.

VEGETABLES: bell pepper (combine different colors—orange, red, and green), yellow onion, scallion, potato, tomato, fennel, sliced mushroom, pencil-thin asparagus.

CHEESE: Gruyère, Emmentaler, Cheddar, Parmigiano-Reggiano, mascarpone, cream cheese, Gorgonzola, feta, fresh goat cheese.

TOPPINGS: Parmigiano-Reggiano, crème fraîche, salsa, sour cream, coarsely cracked pepper, sea salt.

GARNISHES: parsley, watercress, diced tomato, extra filling

Prepare fillings in advance. Sauté, fry, cut, slice, chop, dice, or shred selected meats, vegetables, cheeses, toppings, or garnishes. Put the ingredients in separate bowls and set them aside.

Crack the eggs into a medium mixing bowl. Add water, your favorite fresh chopped herbs, and/or Tabasco. Whisk the eggs to form a frothy, light yellow mixture, 1 to 2 minutes.

Melt the butter with the olive oil in a 10-inch skillet or omelet pan over medium heat. When the butter begins to sizzle but before it turns brown, tip the skillet and allow oil and butter to coat the entire bottom.

Pour the egg into the skillet; it will form a pale yellow disk. Allow the eggs to set; this will take less than a minute. Using a fork, gently lift around the outside edge of the egg disk and tilt the pan so that the uncooked mixture flows underneath.

Beginning with cheese, quickly add the remaining ingredients. Shake the skillet so that the egg disk slides freely. Shake the omelet up to the edge of the skillet and in position to turn out. Fold the omelet over as you slide it onto a warm serving plate.

Blot the omelet with paper towels. Add desired toppings, garnish, and serve.

Yield: 1 to 2 omelets

Eggs Benedict

Hollandaise, a key ingredient in eggs benedict, is a classic French sauce. However, the earliest known recipe for this dish was published in 1894 in the United States. If you're a novice, you're likely to scramble some yolks while learning to make it. Stick with it and you'll soon have the confidence of a celebrity chef. Or, for a foolproof technique, try the blender method below.

> 2 egg yolks
>
> 1½ teaspoons lemon juice
>
> 1½ teaspoons tarragon vinegar
>
> ¼ pound (1 stick) unsalted butter, melted
>
> Kosher salt and cayenne pepper
>
> 2 English muffins, halved and toasted
>
> 4 thick slices Canadian bacon, warmed
>
> 4 eggs
>
> ¼ teaspoon paprika

Heat 1 inch of water in the bottom pan of a double boiler to just under boiling.

Whisk the egg yolks, lemon juice, and vinegar in the top pan of the double boiler until the mixture is bubbly.

Place the top of double boiler over the simmering water and cook the egg mixture, stirring constantly, until the eggs thicken but do not scramble.

Remove the eggs from the heat and drizzle a continuous flow of warm butter into the eggs while whisking the mixture steadily to make a thick sauce. Cover and keep the sauce warm, but not at a temperature where it will cook further.

Add more water to the double boiler and bring it to a boil.

Toast the muffins. Place a slice of Canadian bacon on each muffin half.

Poach the eggs in the hot water. Using a slotted spoon, place the poached eggs on the Canadian bacon. Pour the hollandaise over the eggs. Sprinkle with paprika. Add salt and pepper to taste and serve.

Yield: 2 to 4 servings

Easy Hollandaise

If you have trouble making hollandaise with the traditional double boiler method, break out the blender. Melt the butter completely to 110 degrees. Put the egg yolks, lemon juice, and vinegar in the blender. Cover and blend at high speed. Open the lid and slowly pour in the hot butter while continuing to blend. If the sauce becomes too thick, blend in hot water, a tablespoon at a time, to reach the desired consistency.

Downtown Hash Browns

¼ pound (1 stick) unsalted butter

1 medium onion, coarsely chopped

1½ pounds frozen hash browns, or 3 large Idaho potatoes, peeled and grated

2 cups shredded mozzarella

2 tomatoes, diced

Kosher salt and freshly ground pepper

1½ cups heavy whipping cream

Preheat the oven to 350 degrees.

Melt the butter in a large skillet over medium heat. Add the onions and sauté until they become translucent. Add the potatoes and cook, stirring, until lightly browned and slightly crisp.

Lightly grease a baking pan with shortening. Evenly spread half the cooked potatoes in the pan. Distribute half the cheese and half the diced tomatoes over the potatoes. Sprinkle with salt and pepper. Layer on the remaining potatoes, cheese, and tomatoes, in that order. Lightly sprinkle salt and pepper over the top. Pour the cream evenly over the hash browns.

Bake uncovered for 45 minutes. Remove the pan from the oven and let it sit for 10 to 15 minutes before serving with peppered bacon strips and a fluffy omelet (page 3).

Yield: 6 to 8 servings

Zesty Orange French Toast

In this tasty take on an old classic, tangy orange cream cheese is sandwiched between two layers of Grand Marnier-battered toast. For bolder flavors, try Sicilian blood orange or British bitter orange jam. For texture in the cream cheese, choose a jam with orange zest. Sprinkle with a little powdered sugar and serve with warm Ohio maple syrup.

2 large eggs

1 cup half and half

¼ cup Grand Marnier

1 tablespoon sugar

¼ teaspoon ground cinnamon

½ teaspoon baking powder

1 (4-ounce package) cream cheese, softened

1 tablespoon orange jam

8 extra-thick slices of soft bread

3 tablespoons unsalted butter

¼ cup confectioner's sugar

1 jar raspberry preserves

4 sprigs of fresh mint

Preheat the oven to 350 degrees.

Whisk the eggs, half and half, Grand Marnier, sugar, cinnamon, and baking powder in a bowl until well mixed and slightly foamy.

Blend the cream cheese and jam into a smooth spread in a small bowl. Spread the cream cheese evenly on 4 slices of bread, not quite to the edges of the bread. Place the other 4 slices of bread on top of the cream cheese, so that the slices stick together. Dip each sandwich in the egg bath mixture, turning it once so the bread is completely covered.

Melt the butter in a large skillet or on a griddle over medium heat. Cook the sandwiches, turning once, until light golden brown, 2 to 4 minutes per side.

Place the toast on a cookie sheet and bake it in the oven for 10 minutes.

Slice the toast diagonally. Serve with raspberry preserves spooned in the center. Dust with confectioner's sugar and garnish with mint.

Yield: 4 to 8 servings

Cinnamon Flapjacks

These are the best pancakes I've ever had. If you've never made pancakes from scratch, you'll be amazed at the difference! As a step-saver, sift a double or triple batch of the dry ingredients and store it in an airtight container. The dry mixture will keep until the expiration date on your baking powder. For lighter pancakes, separate the eggs, discard the yolk, then whisk the egg whites and fold them into the batter.

> 2 tablespoons unsalted butter, melted and cooled
> 1 cup all-purpose flour
> 1¼ teaspoon baking powder
> ¼ teaspoon ground cinnamon
> ¼ teaspoon nutmeg
> ¼ teaspoon salt
> 1 large egg
> ¼ cup, plus 2 tablespoons milk
> ¾ cup half and half
> 3 tablespoons light brown sugar
> 1 teaspoon Madagascar bourbon vanilla extract

Melt the butter in a skillet or crepe pan and remove it from the heat.

Sift the flour, baking powder, cinnamon, nutmeg, and salt. Stir the egg into the flour. Add the milk and stir. A very dry batter will begin to form.

Pour in the half and half while continuing to stir until a smooth batter results.

Pour the butter from the skillet into the batter. Add the brown sugar and vanilla. Stir until completely mixed.

Reheat the skillet over medium heat. Pour in enough batter to just fill the bottom. When the pancake's surface bubbles uniformly, flip it and let it cook a few more minutes on the other side. Repeat until all the pancakes are made.

Serve with Ohio maple syrup.

Yield: 7 pancakes

Authentic Crepes

Here's a superb recipe for crepes like those you'll find in a French bistro. You can make these in advance, stack them, cover them tightly with plastic wrap, and then refrigerate or even freeze them. To use, simply let the crepes come back to room temperature. Then they're ready to be stuffed or rolled with any variety of sweet or savory options and reheated in the oven on a baking sheet.

1½ cups all-purpose flour

½ teaspoon salt

½ teaspoon sugar

3 large eggs

1 cup whole milk

3 tablespoons (⅓ stick) unsalted butter, melted

1 tablespoon vegetable oil

1 cup cold water

Combine the flour, salt, and sugar in a mixing bowl. Stir in the eggs. Add the milk and stir until the mixture is smooth. Add the water and the melted butter and whisk until the batter is completely smooth, with no lumps.

Heat a crepe pan over medium heat. Lightly brush the pan with oil. Tilt the pan and pour in 2 tablespoons of batter. Continue to tilt the pan back and forth over the heat to coat the bottom of the pan with batter, forming a thin crepe.

The crepe will be ready to flip when it comes loose as you gently tap the pan against the cooktop. After flipping, cook the crepe for an additional 20 to 30 seconds. Stack the cooked crepes on a plate.

Top or fill and roll the crepes with fresh fruit and whipped cream or ice cream. Glaze them with syrup and dust with powdered sugar.

Yield: 14 crepes

Orange Buttermilk Scones

The orange peel gives these scones a little sunshine on a drizzly northeast Ohio day. This dough keeps well in the refrigerator, or you can cut it into portions and freeze it, making it an easy trick to serve scones straight from the oven on Sunday morning. If you don't have buttermilk, add a tablespoon of lemon juice to just under ¾ cup of milk, mix well, and let stand for five minutes.

3 cups all-purpose flour

3 teaspoons baking powder

1 teaspoon baking soda

1 tablespoon grated orange peel

½ teaspoon salt

¼ cup sugar

¼ pound (1 stick) unsalted butter, melted

1 egg yolk

¾ cup buttermilk

Preheat the oven to 375 degrees.

Using a mixer with a dough hook on low speed, combine the flour, baking powder, soda, orange peel, salt, and sugar.

Add the butter in a slow, steady stream and scrape the sides of the bowl.

Whisk the egg yolk and the buttermilk and add it to the dough mixture in a slow, steady stream. Continue to mix at slow speed until well mixed.

Put the dough on wax paper and roll it out into a ½-inch-thick rectangular shape. Cut the dough first into 4-inch squares, then cut the squares once on the diagonal into triangles. Place the triangles on a cookie sheet.

Bake the scones until they double in height and turn golden brown, 25 to 35 minutes.

Serve with blueberry or raspberry jam.

Yield: 16 scones

Blueberry Breakfast Cakes

These cupcakes are perfect for breakfast. They don't require frosting—just dust them with sugar after they come out of the oven. Depending on what berries are in season, you can substitute raspberries or blackberries, or use a medley of all three.

2 cups sugar

2 tablespoons lemon juice

1 pint fresh blueberries, rinsed

4 eggs, separated

1 cup shortening

2 teaspoons Madagascar bourbon vanilla extract

3 cups all-purpose flour

½ teaspoon salt

2 teaspoons baking powder

½ cup milk

Preheat the oven to 350 degrees.

Stir together ½ cup of the sugar and the lemon juice in a small mixing bowl. Stir in the blueberries. Cover and refrigerate for 2 hours, stirring every 30 minutes.

Beat the egg whites in a small mixing bowl until they hold a stiff peak. Fold in ½ cup of the sugar and set the mixture aside.

Cream the shortening with the remaining 1 cup of sugar with an electric mixer on high speed until the mixture is light and fluffy. Fold in the egg yolks and vanilla, scraping the sides of the bowl.

Sift the flour, salt, and baking powder into a bowl. On a low mixer speed, alternate combining small amounts of the sifted flour and the milk into the creamed shortening.

Carefully fold the egg whites and the blueberries into the cake batter.

Pour the batter into a paper-lined cupcake pan. Bake for 40 minutes.

Yield: 10 to 12 cupcakes

Icebox Coffee Cake

Creaming is a technique that results in better leavening during baking: you beat granulated sugar into solid butter or shortening until it becomes light and fluffy. The volume increases due to the incorporation of air into the mixture. The air bubbles remain in the final batter or dough and expand during baking, helping the cakes or cookies to rise. While butter is the most common fat used for creaming, vegetable shortening is a more effective leavener, as its chemical structure is more conducive to retaining air bubbles at high temperatures.

2¼ cups sifted all-purpose flour

⅓ cup packed dark brown sugar

1 teaspoon cinnamon

6 tablespoons plus ¼ pound (1¾ sticks) unsalted butter, at room temperature

½ cup chopped walnuts

¾ teaspoon baking soda

½ teaspoon baking powder

½ teaspoon salt

⅔ cup sugar

2 large eggs

1 cup sour cream

1 teaspoon Madagascar bourbon vanilla extract

French Buttercream Filling (recipe follows)

Preheat the oven to 325 degrees.

Mix ¾ cup of the flour, the brown sugar, and cinnamon. Using a pastry blender, cut in 6 tablespoons of the butter until the particles are fine. Stir in the walnuts.

Sift the remaining 1½ cups of flour with the baking soda, baking powder, and salt in another bowl and set aside.

Cream the remaining ¼ pound of butter in a large bowl with an electric mixer on high. Gradually add the sugar and beat until light and fluffy.

Scrape the bowl and lower the mixer speed to medium. Add the eggs, one at a time, mixing well after each one. Blend in the vanilla.

Scrape the bowl and set the mixer to low. Alternately spoon in the flour and the sour cream, a little at a time, until all the ingredients are incorporated.

Lightly grease a 9 by 9-inch baking pan with shortening. Pour in the batter. Spread the brown sugar and walnut mix evenly over the batter. Bake until the cake springs back when lightly pressed in the center, 45 to 55 minutes.

Let the cake cool for 10 minutes, then remove it from the pan and let it cool completely. Prepare the buttercream filling while the cake cools.

Cut the cake in half with a serrated knife to make 2 horizontal layers. Generously spread buttercream filling over one layer. Place the other layer on top of the first layer and spread the remaining filling over the top and sides. Cover and refrigerate overnight.

Yield: 8 to 10 servings

French Buttercream Filling

¼ cup all-purpose flour

½ teaspoon salt

1 cup milk

5 ounces (1¼ sticks) unsalted butter, at room temperature

1 cup sugar

1 teaspoon Madagascar bourbon vanilla extract

Combine the flour, salt, and milk in a small saucepan. Stir continuously while cooking over low heat until the mixture is very thick. Let cool.

Cream the butter with an electric mixer on high speed until smooth. Gradually add the sugar and the flour mixture. Beat until light and fluffy. Blend in the vanilla.

Yield: approximately 2½ cups

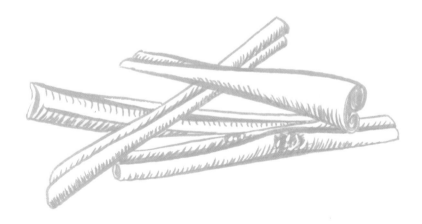

Banana Sour Cream Coffee Cake

Be sure to use a large banana at its ripest stage, with dark, spotted skin and very soft flesh.

1¼ cups sugar

½ cup chopped pecans

1 teaspoon ground cinnamon

¼ teaspoon ground nutmeg

¼ pound (1 stick) unsalted butter, softened

2 large eggs

1 large ripe banana, mashed

½ cup sour cream

½ teaspoon Madagascar bourbon vanilla extract

2 cups all-purpose flour

1 teaspoon baking powder

1 teaspoon baking soda

¼ teaspoon salt

Preheat the oven to 350 degrees.

Stir together ¼ cup of the sugar, the pecans, cinnamon, and nutmeg in a small mixing bowl. Evenly sprinkle half the mixture into 6 well-greased mini Bundt pans or a single 12-cup Bundt pan. Set aside the remaining mixture.

Beat the butter with an electric mixer on medium speed until creamy. Gradually add the remaining 1 cup of sugar, beating an additional 5 to 7 minutes. Scrape the sides of the bowl and beat in the eggs, one at a time. Lower the mixer speed and add the banana, sour cream, and vanilla until the mixture is just blended.

Sift the flour, baking powder, baking soda, and salt in another bowl. Fold the dry mixture into the butter and eggs.

Pour half the batter into the pans. Sprinkle the remaining sugar and cinnamon mixture over the batter. Top with the remaining batter.

Bake until a toothpick inserted into the center of the cake comes out clean, about 45 minutes.

Cool on a wire rack for 10 minutes. Invert the pans and remove the cakes.

Top with a hard sauce or maple glaze.

Yield: 8 to 10 servings

Breakfast on the Verandah

Breads & Sandwiches

NEW YORK CITY is the greatest retail laboratory in the world. In search of the best, authentic New York bagel, our "Foodies," as we like to call our test kitchen crew, searched the shops of Manhattan and found it— boiled, chewy and dense—on West 109th Street. We hired a truck and brought twenty-five cases of fresh, genuine, honest-to-goodness New York bagels to Akron. Bagel lovers from all over town flocked to the store, tasted, and rejected them. Is it possible that they preferred plain old baked bagels that would be laughed off the street in New York? Did they not recognize a good bagel when they saw one? It just goes to show: not everything in Manhattan translates for our customers.

Sweet Potato Biscuits

1 cup (1 medium) dark-skinned sweet potato, mashed

2 cups all-purpose flour

½ teaspoon salt

1 tablespoon baking powder

¼ cup shortening

1 tablespoon grated lemon peel

1 tablespoon grated orange peel

¼ cup honey

½ cup finely chopped crystallized ginger

½ cup half and half

Preheat the oven to 400 degrees.

Peel the sweet potato and place it in a bowl with water. Microwave it on high until fully cooked and soft inside, 10 to 15 minutes. Mash the cooked sweet potato.

Mix the flour, salt, and baking powder in a large bowl. Cut in the shortening.

Stir the lemon and orange peel, honey, ginger, and mashed sweet potato into the flour mixture. Add the half and half while mixing to make a soft dough.

Knead the dough on a floured surface. Pat it down to a thickness of 1 inch. Use a cookie cutter or a glass to make 2½-inch circles of dough. Place the circles of dough on an ungreased cookie sheet.

Bake until light brown, about 15 minutes.

Yield: 12 biscuits

Savory Swiss Muffins

8 slices bacon

2 cups all-purpose flour

2 tablespoons sugar

1 tablespoon baking powder

½ teaspoon salt

¼ pound Gruyère cheese, finely diced

1 large egg

4 tablespoons unsalted butter, melted

2 tablespoons sour cream

1 cup half and half

Preheat the oven to 400 degrees.

Grease a muffin pan or line it with paper cups.

Fry the bacon in a skillet over medium heat until crisp. Drain it on paper towels. Crumble the bacon into fine bits.

Stir together the flour, sugar, baking powder, salt, bacon, and cheese in a large mixing bowl.

Whisk the egg, melted butter, sour cream, and half and half in another bowl. Stir the mixture into the flour until just incorporated. Be careful not to overmix.

Fill the muffin cups three-quarters full.

Bake for 20 minutes.

Yield: 10 to 12 muffins

Rosemary Crisp Bread

For very crisp bread, use a baking stone. If you don't have one, a flat cookie sheet or pizza pan will do. On a baking sheet, the cooking time will be twice as long, ten to fifteen minutes, and the texture of the bread will be slightly different.

¾ cup semolina flour

¾ cup all-purpose flour

¼ teaspoon salt

2½ teaspoons chopped fresh rosemary

⅔ cup water

2 tablespoons extra-virgin olive oil

Coarse sea salt

Parmigiano-Reggiano cheese, shaved

Combine the flours, salt, and rosemary in a large mixing bowl. Mix well. Form a well in the center of the flour mixture and pour in the water and olive oil. Continue mixing with the spoon from the center of the well outward to form the dough.

Remove the dough from the bowl and knead it by hand until smooth, 2 to 3 minutes. Cover the dough with plastic wrap and refrigerate for 1 hour.

Sprinkle a little semolina flour onto the surface of a baking stone and place it on the middle rack of the oven. Heat the oven to 450 degrees.

Divide the chilled dough into six 2-inch balls and cover them loosely with plastic wrap.

On a surface lightly floured with semolina, flatten each ball of dough with the palm of your hand and roll it out into a thin, flat disk.

Transfer the rolled dough to the baking stone and bake until crisp and light golden brown, 5 to 7 minutes.

Remove the bread from the oven and brush both sides generously with olive oil, lightly dusting with sea salt. Top with shavings of Parmigiano-Reggiano cheese. Repeat the process to make about 6 crisp breads.

Yield: 6 flatbreads

Boy Scout Bread

This unusual presentation comes from baking the bread in a coffee can, as a Boy Scout might do over a campfire. Ginger and evaporated milk give the bread a distinctive flavor and texture. Try it lightly toasted with plain or flavored butter.

1 package dry yeast
½ cup warm water (105 to 115 degrees)
3 tablespoons sugar
2 tablespoons vegetable oil
1 teaspoon salt
4½ cups all-purpose flour
⅛ teaspoon ginger
1 (12-ounce) can evaporated milk

Stir the yeast, 1 tablespoon of the sugar, and the oil into the warm water. Let the yeast proof until it foams, 5 to 10 minutes.

Put the flour, salt, the remaining 2 tablespoons of sugar, and the ginger in the bowl of an electric mixer. Using the dough hook attachment, combine the ingredients on low speed, slowly pouring in the evaporated milk.

Continue to mix while slowly pouring in the yeast mixture. Increase the mixer speed slightly and continue mixing until a soft dough is well formed.

Grease the inside of two 1-pound coffee cans with shortening. Put half the dough in each can. Cover the cans with their plastic lids.

Put the cans in a warm area and let the dough rise until it reaches the top of the can, about 1 hour. If the lids pop off while the dough rises, simply push them back down.

Preheat the oven to 350 degrees.

Remove the lids and bake the bread for 45 minutes.

Remove the bread from the oven and let it sit 10 minutes. Gently twist the bread back and forth to remove it from the can. If you wait longer than 10 minutes, the bread will be difficult to remove.

Yield: 2 loaves

Monkey Bread

The story goes that monkey bread was first sold at Neiman Marcus in Dallas in the 1950s. It's difficult to slice this sticky bread, so most people just pull off chunks, like monkeys might do. For extra flavor, we soak the raisins generously in Grand Marnier.

1 cup golden raisins

½ cup Grand Marnier or orange liqueur

1 ½ cups pecans, toasted

½ cup sugar

½ teaspoon freshly grated nutmeg

1 tablespoon cinnamon

¼ pound (1 stick) unsalted butter, melted

1 cup packed dark brown sugar

1 (8-ounce) package cream cheese, softened

2 (12-ounce) tubes refrigerated biscuit dough

Soak the raisins in Grand Marnier in a small bowl for 30 minutes.

Preheat the oven to 350 degrees.

Spread the pecans on a cookie sheet and roast them in the oven until they are oily and golden, about 10 minutes.

Mix the sugar, nutmeg, and cinnamon in a small bowl.

Melt the butter in a small saucepan. Stir in the brown sugar.

Cut the cream cheese into 20 cubes.

Pull apart a portioned biscuit from the tube of dough. Press down the dough with your fingers. Sprinkle the dough with ½ teaspoon of cinnamon sugar. Place a cube of cream cheese in the center of the dough. Add 3 to 4 soaked raisins on top of the cream cheese. Wrap and pinch the dough around the cream cheese and roll it in your hands to form a ball. Repeat this step with all the biscuits.

Grease a 10-cup Bundt pan with shortening or pan spray. Spread ½ cup of the roasted pecans evenly in the bottom of the pan. Evenly distribute half the dough balls in the pan. Sprinkle them with cinnamon sugar. Drizzle ¼ cup of the melted butter over the dough.

Evenly spread another ½ cup of roasted pecans over the dough. Distribute the remaining dough balls in a second layer. Sprinkle on the remaining cinnamon sugar and drizzle on the remaining melted butter. Add the remaining ½ cup of pecans evenly over the top.

Bake the bread for 30 minutes. Remove the pan from the oven and let it cool for 20 minutes before inverting it on a serving plate.

Yield: 10 to 12 servings

Ale House
Grilled Cheese Sandwich

If you can't find farmer's bread, use any dense, firm-textured bread.

3 to 4 tablespoons European butter, softened
2 slices farmer's bread, sliced ⅝-inch thick
¼ pound British onion chive cheese, in thick slices
2 to 3 tablespoons Stonewall Kitchen's farmhouse chutney

Butter the outside of 2 slices of farmer's bread.
Place the cheese slices on the unbuttered side of the bottom slices of bread.
Spread the chutney over the cheese.
Place the remaining slice of bread, butter side up, on top of the cheese.
Cook the sandwich on a griddle or in a skillet over medium-high heat, covered with a lid to melt the cheese.
The sandwich is done when it is golden brown on both sides.

Yield: 1 sandwich

Monte Cristo

The Monte Cristo is a tribute to the stainless-steel diner, an icon from the era of bomb shelters and Ozzie and Harriet on the RCA. While this sandwich's origins are disputed, it was probably inspired by the French croque-monsieur, a grilled ham and Gruyère sandwich.

2 large eggs
¼ cup half and half
Kosher salt and freshly ground pepper
4 tablespoonss (½ stick) unsalted butter, softened
6 pieces ⅜-inch-thick sliced farmer's bread, crust removed
4 thin slices Swiss Emmentaler cheese
4 thin slices rosemary ham
4 thin slices smoked turkey
4 thin slices English farmhouse sharp Cheddar cheese
Confectioner's sugar
Tart cherry jam

Whisk the eggs, half and half, salt, and pepper in a mixing bowl.

Lightly butter both sides of the bread. Build the sandwiches as triple-deckers. Start with a slice of bread, then layer on Swiss, ham, turkey, Cheddar, another slice of bread, Cheddar, turkey, ham, Swiss, and the top slice of bread.

Slice the sandwiches diagonally. Use toothpicks to hold together the layers.

Dip the sandwiches in the egg batter so that all sides are well-coated.

Melt the butter in a skillet over medium heat. Fry the sandwiches until golden brown, 2 to 3 minutes per side. Add more butter to the pan as needed.

Remove the toothpicks and place the sandwiches on warmed individual plates. Dust the tops of the Monte Cristos with confectioner's sugar and spoon a generous dollop of jam on the plate.

Yield: 2 to 4 servings

Curried Chicken Salad Pitas

6 boneless, skinless chicken breast halves

2 teaspoons Madras curry powder

1 cup mayonnaise

2 tablespoons Dijon mustard

2 tart apples, peeled and cored, in ¾-inch cubes

2 celery ribs, diced

1 carrot, chopped

¾ cup dried tart cherries

¼ cup chopped cashews

Kosher salt and freshly ground pepper

4 large pita breads, halved

4 cups mixed salad greens

Slowly poach the chicken breasts in about 1 inch of water in a large skillet over medium-low heat until their internal temperature reaches 165 degrees. Drain the chicken and set it aside to cool. Cut the cooled chicken into ¾-inch cubes.

Toast the curry for 2 minutes in a small skillet over high heat while stirring.

Stir together the mayonnaise, mustard, and toasted curry in a mixing bowl. Add the apples, celery, carrot, cherries, cashews, and chicken. Mix well. Add salt and pepper to taste. Cover tightly and refrigerate until ready to serve.

To assemble the pitas, gently pull apart the cut edge of a pita round, forming a pocket. With the pita on its side, place a bed of lettuce in the pocket. Spoon chicken salad onto the lettuce.

Yield: 8 pitas

Red Pepper Corn Tortillas

With the growing popularity of cuisine from south of the border, flavored pre-made tortillas are easy to find. Still, nothing beats the taste of homemade tortillas fresh from the skillet. Spread them with your favorite fillings and enjoy!

1 cup yellow cornmeal

3 tablespoons all-purpose flour

¼ teaspoon baking soda

1 teaspoon red pepper flakes

¼ teaspoon kosher salt

½ cup buttermilk

1 large egg

Corn oil

1½ cups fresh or frozen corn, thawed

3 scallions, chopped

OPTIONAL FILLINGS:

Chopped tomatoes

Goat cheese

Chopped cilantro

Guacamole

Sour cream

Preheat the oven to 375 degrees.

Stir together the cornmeal, flour, baking soda, red pepper flakes, and salt in a mixing bowl.

In another bowl, whisk the buttermilk and egg until foamy.

Slowly incorporate the wet ingredients into the dry, stirring well each time you add buttermilk mix to the flour mix. Add corn.

Lightly coat a skillet with corn oil and place it on medium heat. When the skillet is hot, pour in just enough tortilla batter to cover the bottom of the pan. Sprinkle scallions evenly on the tortilla. Cook until light brown on both sides, flipping once.

Before serving, quickly reheat the tortillas in a pan over medium heat, flipping once. Cut the tortillas into quarters. Add your favorite ingredients such as chopped tomatoes, goat cheese, cilantro, guacamole, and sour cream, and fold.

Yield: 8 servings

Market Street Deli Wrap

½ cup mayonnaise

2 strips roasted red pepper

½ teaspoon lemon juice

4 large wheat tortillas

½ pound smoked turkey breast, thinly sliced

½ pound smoked ham, thinly sliced

¼ pound provolone cheese, shredded

2 cups romaine lettuce, rinsed and torn

2 small ripe tomatoes, diced

½ small sweet onion, diced

8 slices peppered bacon, cooked and crumbled

Kosher salt and freshly ground pepper

Combine the mayonnaise, red pepper, and lemon juice in a blender and mix until smooth and creamy.

Lightly toast the tortillas in a skillet over medium-high heat, flipping once, about 1 minute per side. Set aside to cool.

Spread a thin layer of pepper mayonnaise evenly over each tortilla. Layer the remaining ingredients on top. To distribute the flavors, alternate between meats and vegetables. Add salt and pepper to taste.

Fold over the bottom quarter of the tortilla. Rotate the tortilla a quarter turn and tightly roll the edge to form a wrap.

Yield: 4 wraps

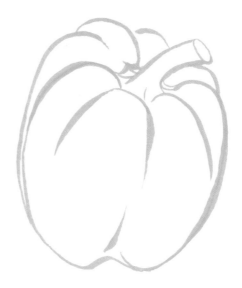

Pulled Chicken Wrap

For this easy but tasty lunch dish, we use the cooked rotisserie chicken you can find in most delis and supermarkets. Spread your favorite spicy salsa or fresh guacamole over the filling for added flavor.

1 cut-up roasted chicken (page 154) or cooked rotisserie chicken

½ cup spicy prepared salsa

8 large tortilla or lavash wraps

2 tablespoons chopped fresh cilantro

2 scallions, thinly sliced

1 yellow bell pepper, chopped

1 red bell pepper, chopped

½ pound Montrachet or other goat cheese, crumbled

½ pound of pepper jack cheese, shredded

4 large button mushrooms, washed and thinly sliced

Pull the meat off the chicken bones and pull it apart to make bite-sized pieces.

Spread a thin layer of salsa on a tortilla. Lightly sprinkle the cilantro and scallions over the salsa.

Distribute the chicken, peppers, cheeses, and mushrooms evenly in layers on the tortilla. Leave the top and bottom 2 inches of the tortilla free of toppings. Be careful not to overload the tortilla, or it will be difficult to roll it closed.

Fold the top and bottom of the tortilla over the ingredients. Rotate the tortilla a quarter turn and roll the filled tortilla to make a tight wrap. Cut it diagonally in half to serve.

Yield: 8 wraps

Appetizers

THESE DAYS when we spend time at our lake house, my wife gets to vacation and I get to cook. I call it playing. I have a studio there where I paint, but before mealtimes I indulge in my other favorite art form. I combine flavors, try new ingredients, experiment, or clean out the refrigerator to make a soup, salad, or omelet. I spend my creative energy on our meals, so when it comes to appetizers, I like to keep it simple. I make sure to stock our shelves with the best West Point Market offers, keeping my favorites—Mama Lil's roasted red peppers (one of the thirty-six ingredients for sandwiches), cute little red Peppadews for stuffing, chutneys and pâtés, and always some good crusty bread.

Brie en Croûte

Puff pastry consists of multiple layers of dough with butter between them. Baking makes the pastry rise dramatically into a flaky, airy, buttery crust. Croissants are a classic example of a baked puff pastry. Don't confuse puff pastry dough with phyllo dough—the latter consists of tissue-thin layered dough sheets and is used for Mediterranean pastries like baklava. You'll find puff pastry sheets and phyllo dough sold in the freezer case at better food stores.

1 (14-ounce) package frozen puff pastry dough

1 (12-ounce) jar pear preserves

1 (2-pound) wheel double-cream Brie

2 eggs, beaten

1 French baguette, sliced and toasted

Preheat the oven to 375 degrees.

Thaw the puff pastry and roll it out into a square.

Put the preserves in the center of the dough and spread them out to a circle of the same diameter as the Brie. Place the Brie on top of the preserves. Trim off four corners of dough and reserve them for garnish.

Brush beaten egg on the dough. Fold the edges of the dough over the Brie. Cover a baking sheet with parchment paper. Flip over the Brie and put it on the baking sheet.

Brush some more beaten egg on the dough. Garnish the pastry with strips of dough in fancy cuts, curls, or twists.

Bake the dough to a golden brown color, about 20 minutes.

Serve on a platter accompanied with toasted slices of baguette.

Yield: 12 to 16 servings

Baked Brie and Apples

½ cup dark brown sugar

½ cup chopped pecans

1 pound double-cream Brie

2 Granny Smith apples, sliced into thin wedges

1 French baguette

Preheat the broiler.

Toss the dark brown sugar and chopped pecans in a bowl until well mixed.

Put the Brie in a metal pan or Pyrex dish. Heap the sugar and pecan mixture on top.

Place the Brie under the broiler until the sugar melts and the pecans are toasted. Be careful not to let the sugar burn.

Remove the Brie from the pan with a spatula. Serve it with sliced baguette and apples.

Yield: 6 to 8 servings

Fried Brie with
Spicy Apricot Salsa

Although some artisan Brie cheese is now crafted in northern California, classic Brie comes from the cows of France. French Brie is available in double-cream and triple-cream varieties; the difference is in the butterfat content. Under French law, triple-cream has a minimum of 75 percent butterfat while double-cream has at least 60 percent.

At the peak of ripeness, Brie is very soft and actually oozes. For this recipe, choose a slightly younger, firmer double-cream Brie that will hold up better when you peel and fry it.

1 half-pound wedge French Brie cheese

1 egg, beaten

1 cup fine panko breadcrumbs

1 tablespoon sunflower oil

1 small onion, finely chopped

1 small fresh hot pepper, seeded and finely chopped

1 poblano chile pepper, seeded and finely chopped

¾ cup finely chopped dried apricots

⅔ cup orange juice

Vegetable oil for frying

Fresh salad leaves, for garnish

Scrape or cut away the white rind from the Brie. Cut the Brie into 4 equal wedges.

Dip the Brie in the beaten egg and coat it with breadcrumbs.

Cover the cheese and put it in the refrigerator while preparing the salsa.

Heat the sunflower oil in a skillet and gently sauté the onions and peppers for 5 minutes over medium heat. Add the apricots and orange juice and simmer until thick and chunky, about 15 minutes.

Heat the vegetable oil in a deep skillet or fryer. Fry the Brie until golden, 2 to 3 minutes. Drain it on paper towels.

Place the Brie on a serving dish. Garnish with salad leaves and serve with apricot salsa.

Yield: 2 to 4 servings

Roquefort Butter Ball

European butter is slightly richer and drier than its American counterpart, with 82 to 86 percent butterfat content, while most American brands of butter have about 80 percent butterfat. The difference may seem small but the fuller flavor is striking in this cheese ball.

¾ pound softened European butter

½ cup softened Roquefort cheese

2 teaspoons Dijon mustard

2 tablespoons brandy

1 cup hazelnuts

Preheat the oven to 350 degrees.

Mix the butter, cheese, mustard, and brandy. Put the mixture in the refrigerator to cool slightly.

Chop the hazelnuts and spread them on a baking sheet. Toast them in the oven until brown, about 10 minutes. Let cool.

Remove the butter and cheese mixture from the refrigerator and form it into a ball. Put the hazelnuts in a bowl and roll the cheese ball around until the nuts completely cover its surface.

Place the cheese ball on a serving dish and cover with plastic wrap. Keep it in the refrigerator until ready to serve.

Yield: 6 to 8 servings

Five-Cheese Cheesecake

¾ cup panko breadcrumbs

1 tablespoon pine nuts

3 tablespoons extra-virgin olive oil

¼ teaspoon dried basil

¼ teaspoon dried thyme

¼ teaspoon dried oregano

1 pound cream cheese, at room temperature

1 large egg

¼ pound brie cheese, rind removed, at room temperature

¼ pound chèvre cheese, at room temperature

¼ cup pecorino Romano cheese, grated

¼ pound Gorgonzola cheese, at room temperature

Pinch of salt

Pinch of ground white pepper

1½ cups heavy whipping cream

Preheat the oven to 350 degrees.

Stir together the breadcrumbs, pine nuts, olive oil, basil, thyme, and oregano in a mixing bowl until well blended. Transfer the mixture to a 6-inch springform pan. Pat the mixture over the bottom of the pan to form an even crust.

Cream the cream cheese with a mixer on high speed until smooth. On medium speed, mix in the egg, brie, chèvre, Romano, Gorgonzola, salt, and pepper. Slowly add the heavy cream, stirring until the mixture is smooth.

Pour the cheese mixture into the springform pan. Bake until golden brown on top, about 40 minutes.

Remove the cheesecake from the oven and let it cool. Refrigerate it until ready to serve.

Yield: 8 to 10 slices

French Ham and Onion Tart

"Jambon" is the French word for ham. However, the French variety is a whole-muscle ham encased in a layer of fat. After salt-curing, it is either poached, yielding a moister ham, or smoked for a denser consistency. The jambon you're likely to find in the United States, including that in our deli department, is imported from Canada. You can substitute baked ham in this recipe.

½ teaspoon sugar

1 cup warm water (105–115 degrees)

1 package (1 teaspoon) active dry yeast

2¼ cups all-purpose flour

½ teaspoon fine sea salt

¾ cup crème fraîche (recipe follows)

⅓ cup large curd cottage cheese

⅓ cup sour cream

Salt and freshly ground pepper

½ large Vidalia or other sweet onion, thinly sliced

2 shallots, chopped

12 ounces ¼-inch-thick sliced jambon, cubed

1 cup smoked Gouda cheese, shredded

Completely dissolve the sugar in the warm water. Stir in the yeast until dissolved. Let the mixture develop a ½-inch foam on top. Note: the yeast will not leaven the flour unless the temperature is between 105 degrees and 115 degrees.

Combine the flour and sea salt in a mixing bowl. Form a well in the center of the flour and add the yeast mixture. Stir from the center of the well outward to form a slightly sticky dough. If the mixture is too sticky, knead in extra flour, one tablespoon at a time. Cover tightly with plastic wrap and let the dough rise for 1½ hours.

Preheat the oven to 450 degrees.

Blend the crème fraîche, cottage cheese, and sour cream in a food processor until smooth. Add salt and pepper to taste.

Lightly flour your hands and punch down the dough. Cut the dough in half. Roll out each half on a lightly floured surface into a 10 by 16-inch rectangle. Put each sheet of dough onto separate, lightly floured baking sheets.

Spread half the cream mixture evenly over each sheet of dough, leaving uncovered a half inch of dough around the edge. Mix the onions, shallots, ham, and Gouda, and sprinkle them evenly over the cream mixture.

Bake the tarts until the edge of the crust is crisp and golden brown, about 15 minutes.

Yield: Either two 10 by 16-inch flat tarts on a baking sheet (6 servings), or four 8-inch round tarts

Crème Fraîche

1 cup heavy whipping cream
1 cup sour cream
2 tablespoons buttermilk

Whisk the whipping cream and the sour cream with the buttermilk. Cover the bowl and leave it at room temperature for up to 24 hours, to allow it to thicken. Keep the covered bowl in the refrigerator for another 4 to 8 hours before using.

Yield: 2 cups

Creamy Crab and Cheese Mini Muffins

2 cups all-purpose flour

1½ teaspoons baking powder

1½ teaspoons baking soda

½ teaspoon salt

1 large egg

⅔ cup plain yogurt

⅔ cup sour cream

½ cup finely chopped fresh parsley

¼ cup finely chopped dill

¼ cup chopped sun-dried tomatoes

2 ounces sharp Cheddar cheese, grated

7 ounces "special" grade blue crab meat, cooked and flaked

2 tablespoons mayonnaise or Aioli

1 (8-ounce) package cream cheese

Kosher salt and freshly ground pepper

Preheat the oven to 400 degrees.

Sift the flour, baking powder, baking soda, and salt in a large bowl.

Beat the egg until foamy in another bowl. Stir in the yogurt, sour cream, parsley, dill, sun-dried tomatoes, and cheese.

Stir the egg mixture into the flour. Do not overmix.

Spoon the batter into mini muffin tins or a greased muffin pan and bake for 20 minutes.

While the muffins cool, flake the crab meat in a mixing bowl. Stir in the mayonnaise and cream cheese. Add salt and pepper to taste.

Cut the cooled muffins in half, fill with the crab mix, and serve.

Yield: 24 muffins

Potted Shrimp

2 tablespoons olive oil

1 clove garlic, chopped

1 pound shrimp, any size, peeled and deveined

½ pound (2 sticks) unsalted butter

1 tablespoon Dijon mustard

2 tablespoons lemon juice

½ teaspoon celery salt

1 teaspoon salt

¼ teaspoon freshly ground pepper

1 French baguette

Extra-virgin olive oil

¼ cup chopped parsley

Sauté the garlic in olive oil a small skillet over medium heat until it just begins to brown. Add the shrimp and stir until they are pink and cooked through. Place the mixture in a food processor or blender. Add the butter, mustard, lemon juice, celery salt, salt and pepper. Blend the ingredients until well mixed and the shrimp is cut into fine pieces.

Cover and chill for 4 hours.

Preheat the oven to 350 degrees.

Thinly slice the baguette and brush the slices lightly with olive oil. Place the slices on a baking sheet, oil side up, and toast in the oven until lightly golden. Remove them from the oven and let cool.

To serve, spread the potted shrimp on the toast and garnish with a pinch of fresh parsley.

Yield: 8 to 10 servings

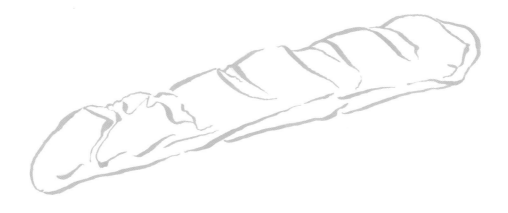

Shrimp Cocktail

1 cup ketchup

2 tablespoons Worcestershire sauce

2 tablespoons lemon juice

1 teaspoon freshly ground horseradish, plus additional to taste

3 drops Tabasco

¼ teaspoon celery salt

¼ teaspoon salt

¼ teaspoon freshly ground pepper

12 jumbo shrimp, cooked, peeled, and deveined

Stir the ingredients in a small bowl until well mixed. To increase the spiciness or heat, add more horseradish, a teaspoon at a time.

Arrange the shrimp on a tray with a bowl of cocktail sauce in the center.

Yield: 4 to 6 servings

Spinach Artichoke Dip

This is a favorite from our deli case. For a more complex, granular texture, use aged Parmigiano-Reggiano instead of Asiago. While best when fresh, this dip will keep overnight if you refrigerate it in a tightly sealed container.

1 cup heavy cream

2 (8-ounce) packages cream cheese

½ cup aged Asiago cheese, shredded

3 tablespoons cornstarch

1 (10-ounce) package chopped spinach, thawed

1 (12-ounce) can quartered artichokes, drained

½ cup finely shredded carrot

¼ cup sliced water chestnuts, drained

¼ teaspoon cayenne pepper

Salt and freshly ground pepper

Heat the heavy cream and cream cheese in a saucepan over medium heat, stirring until the cream cheese melts. Stir in the Asiago cheese until melted. Mix the cornstarch in a little water, then stir it into the saucepan until the mixture thickens. Remove the pan from the heat.

Stir in the spinach, artichokes, carrots, water chestnuts, and cayenne pepper until they are well incorporated throughout the mixture.

Salt and pepper to taste.

Yield: 7 cups

Maryland Crab Dip

We prefer backfin crab, a mix of smaller pieces of jumbo lump crab and larger pieces of body meat. For a smoother consistency, use "special" grade—smaller flakes from the body of the crab. Choose a fruity, extra-virgin olive oil or substitute one where the olives were pressed with lemon peel. Leave out the lemon juice if you use lemon oil. Have some fun selecting the Cheddar—taste a few English farmhouse samples at your cheese shop. Pick one that is relatively low in moisture, with complex flavors.

1 French baguette

Extra-virgin olive oil

¼ cup chopped fresh parsley leaves

2 (8-ounce) packages cream cheese, softened

1 cup sour cream

¼ cup mayonnaise

1 tablespoon Worcestershire sauce

1 tablespoon lemon juice

1 teaspoon dry mustard

¼ teaspoon garlic powder

½ teaspoon kosher salt

1 pound backfin or mixed "special" grade crab meat, cooked

2 tablespoons chopped fresh chives

¼ pound sharp English farmhouse Cheddar cheese, shredded

Preheat the oven to 350 degrees.

Thinly slice the baguette and place the slices on a cookie sheet. Brush the bread lightly with olive oil. Toast the bread in the oven until it just turns light golden brown. Remove the toasts from the oven and sprinkle them lightly with chopped parsley.

Beat the cream cheese and sour cream with an electric mixer until light and smooth. With the mixer on low, add the mayonnaise, Worcestershire sauce, lemon juice, mustard, garlic powder, and salt.

Fold in the crab meat and chives.

Transfer the crab mixture to a baking dish. Spread the Cheddar cheese evenly on top. Bake for 35 minutes on the middle oven rack. Serve the dip warm with the baguette toasts.

Yield: 8 to 10 servings

Candied Ginger Fruit Dip

1½ cups sour cream

2 tablespoons brown sugar

3 tablespoons candied ginger pieces

½ cup apricot or peach preserves

Mix the ingredients in a bowl and stir until well blended. Cover and refrigerate for at least ½ hour.

Yield: 2 cups

Award-Winning Salsa

1 (28-ounce) can diced tomatoes, drained

1 (4-ounce) can diced green chilies, drained

1 (4-ounce) can diced jalapeño peppers, drained

1 large onion, chopped

½ clove garlic, diced

2 yellow bell peppers, chopped

6 ripe strawberries, chopped

1 bunch cilantro leaves, chopped

¼ teaspoon salt

1 teaspoon freshly ground pepper

¼ cup balsamic vinegar

1 teaspoon lime juice

Mix the ingredients in a small bowl until well blended. Cover tightly and refrigerate for 2 to 4 hours. To make a silky, smooth dip or topping, purée the salsa in a blender or food processor.

Yield: 6 cups

Tex-Mex Barbecue

Award-Winning Salsa with Tortilla Chips   46

Grilled Shrimp and Asparagus Salad   80
Sauvignon Blanc, St. Supéry, Napa Valley, California

Red Mole Rotisserie Chicken   156
Garnacha Viña Borgia, Bodegas Borsao, Campo de Borja, Spain

Mixed Grilled Vegetables   126

Sweet Potato Biscuits   19

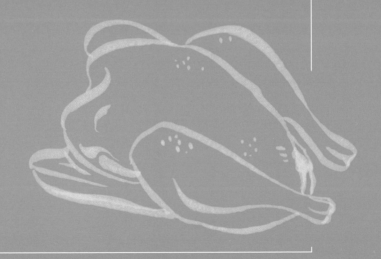

Soups

MANY SOUPS were born of the need to clean out the fridge, giving our test kitchen a chance to perform fun experiments with the products on hand, using seasonal fruits and vegetables when possible. In the summer, we offer light, cold soups such as gazpachos or Scandinavian fruit soups. In the winter, we serve heavier fare: creamy soups, chilis, or brothy, garnished soups such as minestrone. Although some might argue that authentic chili does not have noodles, I find that adding mini penne or small shells turns it in to a hearty meal, perfect for a winter day.

My favorite soups are good hearty clam chowders and chicken noodle soup. Now that I am watching my weight and have to stay away from heavier foods, I prefer the chicken noodle. It always seems to bring back the smell and flavor of home. That's why we always serve chicken noodle soup in our café any time of the year. It's tradition.

Chicken Noodle Soup

½ pound boneless, skinless chicken thighs
½ pound boneless, skinless chicken breast
1 tablespoon unsalted butter
⅓ cup diced celery
⅓ cup diced onion
⅓ cup sliced carrot
¼ teaspoon dried thyme leaf
¼ teaspoon dried parsley
5 cups water
4 teaspoons chicken base
¾ cup medium dry egg noodles
¼ teaspoon ground white pepper

Preheat the oven to 350 degrees.

Put the chicken thighs and breasts on a parchment-lined baking pan. Bake the chicken for 10 minutes each side, turning once. Remove the chicken from the oven and let it cool. Dice the chicken into ½-inch cubes.

Sauté the celery, onions, and carrots in the butter in a stockpot over medium heat until slightly tender.

Add the thyme, parsley, water, and chicken base. Simmer the mixture for 15 minutes.

Add the noodles, diced chicken, and pepper. When the noodles are tender, lower the heat and let the soup simmer an additional 5 to 7 minutes.

Yield: 6 1-cup servings

Cheesy Chicken and Artichoke Soup

4 tablespoons (½ stick) unsalted butter

2 carrots, chopped

2 celery stalks, sliced

1 medium onion, chopped

2 cloves garlic, minced

2 (14-ounce) cans chicken broth

½ teaspoon kosher salt

½ teaspoon ground white pepper

2 cups half and half

¼ cup all-purpose flour

1½ cups cubed cooked chicken breast

1 cup heavy cream

½ cup artichoke hearts, drained and cut into small pieces

½ cup frozen chopped spinach, thawed and well drained

¼ pound Brie cheese, rind removed

Melt the butter in a stock pot over medium heat. Sauté the carrots, celery, onion, and garlic until the onions become translucent.

Add the broth, salt, and pepper. Continue stirring until the soup comes to a boil. Lower the heat and simmer for 15 minutes.

Add ¼ cup of the half and half to the flour and stir the mixture until smooth. Add the remaining 1¾ cups of half and half and stir until the flour batter is well mixed, with no lumps. Pour the batter into the soup and stir until thickened.

Stir in the chicken, cream, artichoke, spinach, and brie. Cook the soup until the cheese is completely melted, about 5 minutes.

Yield: 4 to 8 servings

High Country Stew

¼ cup extra-virgin olive oil plus extra for sautéing

1½ teaspoons herbes de Provence

½ teaspoon kosher salt

½ teaspoon freshly ground pepper

2½–3 pounds boneless leg of lamb, cut into 1-inch cubes

½ pound thickly sliced bacon

1 medium onion, finely chopped

1½ cups water

2 cups brewed coffee

3 tablespoons Tabasco

2 tablespoons molasses

2 tablespoons Worcestershire sauce

12 shallots, peeled and halved

12 small red potatoes, unpeeled, halved

4 carrots, chopped

¼ cup chopped fresh parsley

Kosher salt and freshly ground pepper

Blend ¼ cup olive oil, herbes de Provence, salt, and pepper in a mixing bowl. Add the lamb and stir to coat the meat. Cover the bowl tightly with plastic wrap and refrigerate overnight.

Fry the bacon in a skillet over medium heat until crisp. Drain it on paper towels. Cut the bacon into ½-inch slices and set it aside.

Cook the lamb in the bacon drippings, turning the pieces frequently, until browned on all sides. Put the cooked lamb on a plate and set it aside.

Sauté the chopped onion in a stockpot in a little olive oil over medium heat until the onion becomes soft. Add the water, coffee, Tabasco, molasses, and Worcestershire sauce and bring to a boil. Lower the heat and add the shallots, potatoes, carrots, bacon, and lamb. Cover and simmer for 2½ hours, stirring occasionally.

Stir in the parsley and season to taste with salt and pepper.

Yield: 6 to 12 servings

Suggested wine: Côtes du Rhône Blanc, Guigal, Southern Rhône, France

Beef, Vegetable, and Barley Stew

3 tablespoons olive oil

Meat from 4 crosscut beef shanks, cubed

1 large onion, chopped

2 garlic cloves, minced

4 cups beef stock

¼ cup red wine

5 carrots, sliced

1 (28-ounce) can crushed whole tomatoes, drained

⅔ cup barley

½ pound fresh green beans, quartered

2 cups fresh or frozen sweet corn

6 small red potatoes, cubed

1 stalk celery, sliced

¼ cabbage, chopped

8 ounces frozen peas

1 teaspoon oregano

Kosher salt and freshly ground pepper

¼ cup grated Parmigiano-Reggiano cheese

Sauté the shanks in oil in a stock pot over medium-high heat until browned, stirring occasionally. Add the onion and garlic and sauté until the onion becomes soft.

Add the beef stock, wine, carrots, tomatoes, barley, and oregano. Bring to a boil, then lower the heat and simmer for 1½ hours.

Stir in the green beans, corn, potatoes, celery, and cabbage and simmer for 1 hour. Add the peas during the last ½ hour. Add salt and pepper to taste.

Serve hot with grated cheese.

Yield: 6 to 12 servings

Potato, Bacon, and Leek Soup

2 thick slices bacon

1 leek, sliced thin

¼ cup diced onion

2 cups chicken broth

1 pound Yukon gold potatoes, peeled and cut into ¾-inch cubes

¼ cup shredded Gruyère cheese

¼ teaspoon salt

½ teaspoon freshly ground pepper

1 tablespoon chopped parsley

Fry the bacon in a stock pot over medium heat until crisp. Drain it on paper towels.

Sauté the leeks and onion in the bacon drippings until tender, about 5 minutes. Add the broth and potatoes. Stir and bring to a boil. Lower the heat, cover, and simmer for 10 minutes.

Using a slotted spoon, remove 1 cup of potatoes. Mash together the potatoes and Gruyère in a small mixing bowl until the cheese melts and the potatoes are smooth. Stir the potato mixture back into the soup.

Crumble the bacon. Add the bacon, salt, and pepper to the soup and mix well.

Serve the soup in bowls garnished with parsley.

Yield: 3 to 6 servings

Minestrone

Minestrone means "big soup" and there are as many variations as there are families who make it. Although our recipe includes prosciutto, you could use beef shanks, stew meat, or even roaster chicken in this Italian soup.

¼ cup extra-virgin olive oil

2 cloves garlic, chopped

½ cup diced red onion

½ cup diced leek

2 carrots, peeled and diced

2 celery stalks, diced

¼ pound prosciutto di Parma, sliced ½-inch thick and diced

5 cups beef broth

1 cup peeled and diced red potato

¼ pound Swiss chard, rinsed and chopped

½ cup diced plum tomatoes

1 zucchini, diced

¼ cup cooked white kidney (cannellini) beans, drained

¼ pound tubetti or other small pasta

¼ cup prepared pesto sauce

Freshly ground pepper

¼ cup freshly grated Parmigiano-Reggiano cheese

Sauté the garlic, onion, leeks, carrot, celery, and prosciutto in a stock pot over medium heat until the onion becomes translucent, about 5 minutes.

Add the broth, potatoes, Swiss chard, tomatoes, zucchini, and beans and bring to a boil while stirring. Lower the heat, cover, and simmer for 15 minutes, stirring occasionally.

Stir in the tubetti and cook until the pasta is al dente. Drain the pasta and return it to the pot. Stir in the pesto.

Serve in individual bowls with pepper and Parmigiano-Reggiano cheese and a thick slice of crusty bread on the side.

Yield: 4 to 8 servings

Suggested wine: Sicilia Rosso, Cantine Colosi, Sicily, Italy

Pasta Fagioli

This is a hearty Italian soup of pasta, beans (fagioli), and dry-cured ham. The first-generation Italian-American families who popularized this dish often combined Saturday's leftover marinara sauce with pasta and cannellini beans to create an inexpensive weekday meal. We use ground veal but, in keeping with tradition, you could use leftover meatballs or sausage. If you have a favorite pasta sauce, simplify this recipe by substituting your sauce for the tomatoes, tomato sauce, tomato juice, salt, pepper, oregano, basil, and thyme (about 3½ cups of pasta sauce), and salt and pepper the soup to taste.

    1 tablespoon extra-virgin olive oil

    2 cloves garlic, very thinly sliced

    1 medium onion, diced

    1 small carrot, sliced into thin strips

    3 stalks celery, thinly sliced

    1 pound ground veal

    1 (28-ounce) can San Marzano tomatoes, drained and crushed

    1 cup tomato sauce

    1 cup tomato juice

    1 cup red kidney beans, rinsed and drained

    1 cup white kidney (cannellini) beans, rinsed and drained

    1 tablespoon vinegar

    1½ teaspoons kosher salt

    ½ teaspoon freshly ground pepper

    1 teaspoon chopped fresh oregano

    1 teaspoon chopped fresh basil

    ½ teaspoon fresh thyme

    ½ pound tubetti or other small pasta

    ¼ pound Asiago cheese, grated

Sauté the garlic in olive oil in a stock pot over medium heat until it just begins to brown. Add the onion, carrot, celery, and ground veal. Continue to sauté, stirring, until the veal is browned, about 10 minutes. Drain the mixture in a colander to remove the fat.

Put the veal mixture back in the stock pot and return the pan to medium heat. Stir in the tomatoes, tomato sauce, tomato juice, beans, vinegar, 1 teaspoon of the salt, the pepper, oregano, basil, and thyme. Bring to a boil, lower the heat, and cover. Simmer for 1 hour.

Bring a large pot of water to a boil. Stir in the remaining 3 teaspoons of salt and the pasta. Boil until al dente. Drain the pasta.

Gently stir the cooked pasta into the soup. Serve in individual bowls with grated Asiago cheese and a thick slice of crusty bread on the side.

Yield: 4 to 8 servings

Suggested wine: Centine-Sangiovese/Cabernet Sauvignon/Merlot, Banfi, Tuscany, Italy

Navy Bean and Vegetable Soup

4 strips peppered bacon

1 large onion, chopped

2 cloves garlic, minced

1 bay leaf

1 teaspoon fresh thyme leaf

1 pound fingerling potatoes, cut into ¾-inch pieces

4 carrots, sliced into ½-inch pieces

3 turnips, peeled, halved and sliced

1½ cups chicken broth

½ cup dry white wine

3 (15-ounce) cans navy beans, drained

½ teaspoon kosher salt

½ teaspoon freshly ground pepper

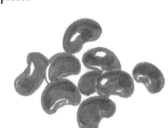

Fry the bacon in a skillet over medium heat until crisp. Drain it on paper towels.

Sauté the onion and garlic in the bacon drippings until the garlic just begins to brown, about 3 minutes.

Crumble the bacon and put it in a crock pot. Using a slotted spoon, add the garlic and onion to the crock pot. Add the bay leaf, thyme, potatoes, carrots, turnips, broth, wine, beans, salt, and pepper. Mix well.

Set the crock pot on high and cook for 1 hour. Lower the heat and slow—cook, stirring occasionally, until the vegetables are soft, 6 to 7 hours.

Yield: 3 to 6 servings

Lentil Soup

2 thick slices bacon

1 tablespoon extra-virgin olive oil

2 cloves garlic, minced

2 scallions with tops, chopped

6 cups chicken stock

1 teaspoon finely chopped fresh thyme

1 bay leaf

1 pound brown lentils

Fry the bacon in a saucepan over medium heat until crisp. Drain it on paper towels.

Add olive oil and sauté the garlic and scallions until the garlic is light brown and the scallions are soft.

Add the chicken stock, thyme, bay leaf, and lentils. Bring to a boil while stirring. Cover, lower the heat, and simmer until the lentils are tender, 35 to 40 minutes.

Yield: 4 to 8 servings

Split Pea Soup

2 cloves garlic, minced

1 medium onion, minced

4 celery ribs, chopped

2 tablespoons olive oil

½ pound dried split peas, rinsed

4 cups chicken stock

3 carrots, diced

½ pound smoked ham, diced

½ pound bacon

½ pound frozen peas

¼ cup chopped flat-leaf parsley

Sauté the garlic, onion and celery in oil in a stock pot over medium heat until the garlic is soft and light brown. Add the dried peas, chicken stock, carrots, and ham and bring to a boil. Lower the heat and simmer for 1 ½ hours, stirring occasionally.

Fry the bacon in a skillet over medium heat until crisp. Drain it on paper towels.

Crumble the bacon and add it to the soup. Add the frozen peas and simmer ½ hour.

Stir in the parsley and serve with crusty bread. The soup may be refrigerated or frozen.

Yield: 4 to 8 servings

White Asparagus Soup

Once a local springtime treat, today fresh asparagus is available year-round. At West Point Market, we continue to have passionate debates about whether asparagus is best when it is thick and meaty, or when it has delicate pencil-thin stalks. This recipe calls for white asparagus, which tends to be thicker. Like mushrooms, white asparagus is grown commercially, without any sunlight.

6 ounces (1½ sticks) unsalted butter

1 clove garlic, minced

1 medium onion, chopped

6 cups chicken stock

6 cups water

¼ cup lemon juice

2 tablespoons sugar

1 teaspoon kosher salt

1 pound fresh white asparagus, bottoms removed and discarded

1 medium potato, peeled and cut into ½-inch pieces

1 cup heavy cream

Salt and freshly ground pepper

Sauté the garlic and onion in a stock pot with ½ stick of the butter until the onion becomes soft.

Add the chicken stock, water, lemon juice, sugar, and salt and bring to a boil.

Add the aparagus spears and cook until tender. Remove the asparagus and drain it in a colander. Slice the spears into 1-inch pieces and set aside.

Add the potato and continue to boil the stock mixture until reduced by one third.

Lower the heat and stir in the cream, the remaining stick of butter, and the sliced asparagus. Simmer for 15 minutes. Add salt and pepper to taste.

Yield: 6 to 12 servings

West Point Vegetable Soup

½ pound dried white kidney (cannellini) beans

2 tablespoons extra-virgin olive oil

½ large onion, finely chopped

2 cloves garlic, minced

1 tablespoon chopped fresh thyme

½ cup chopped green cabbage

1 (14½-ounce) can diced plum tomatoes, drained

2 celery stalks, cut into ½-inch pieces

2 carrots, cut into ½-inch pieces

5 cups vegetable broth or stock

1 medium potato, cut into ½-inch pieces

¼ cup chopped fresh basil

1 cup chopped red cabbage

2 medium zucchini, cut into ½-inch pieces

½ cup grated pecorino Romano cheese

Freshly ground pepper

Extra-virgin olive oil

Put the beans in a pot and cover them with water. Cover the pot. Refrigerate and soak the beans overnight. Drain the beans.

Sauté the onion and garlic in a stock pot over medium heat until the garlic just begins to brown. Add the thyme, cabbage, tomatoes, celery, and carrots. Cook for 10 minutes, stirring occasionally.

Add the beans, vegetable broth, potatoes, and basil. Stir while bringing to a boil. Lower the heat, cover, and simmer for 1 hour.

Add the red cabbage and zucchini. Cover and simmer for another 20 minutes.

Remove the soup from the heat and stir in the cheese.

Ladle the soup into bowls, add a pinch of ground pepper, and drizzle with olive oil.

Yield: 4 to 8 servings

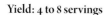

Baja Corn Soup

4 cups fresh or frozen sweet corn

1 cup half and half

¼ cup lime juice

1 tablespoon extra-virgin olive oil

1 clove garlic, chopped

1 large red onion, diced

2 dried poblano chili peppers, seeded and diced

2 cups chicken broth

1 teaspoon kosher salt

½ teaspoon cayenne pepper

1½ cups diced tomato, drained

¼ cup grated Cotija Queso cheese

¼ cup chopped fresh cilantro

Combine 2 cups of the corn, the half and half, and lime juice in a blender.

Sauté the garlic and onion in a stockpot over medium heat until the garlic just begins to brown, about 3 minutes. Add the chilies, broth, the remaining 2 cups of corn, the salt, and pepper. Bring to a boil while stirring.

Lower the heat and stir in the blended corn and cream mixture and the diced tomato. Cover and simmer for 15 minutes.

Serve in individual bowls with grated cheese and fresh cilantro on top.

Yield: 3 to 6 servings

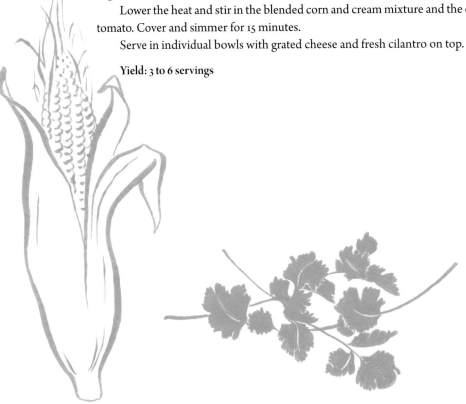

Red Chil

Our made-from-scratch chili is a longtime winter favorite at West Point Market. After Texas, Ohio is the chili capital of North America, largely because of the popularity of Cincinnati chili. This recipe should be served with plenty of mild shredded Cheddar cheese on top. For a Cincinnati flair, ladle your chili over spaghetti and top it with a heaping mound of cheese.

> 2 pounds ground sirloin
> 1 (28-ounce) can crushed tomatoes
> 2 (15-ounce) cans tomato sauce
> 2 (16-ounce) cans dark red kidney beans
> ½ large onion, chopped
> 1 tablespoon chili powder
> 1 teaspoon dry mustard
> 1 teaspoon kosher salt
> 1 large bay leaf
> 1 cup grated Cheddar cheese
> Sour Cream Topping (recipe follows)

Brown the ground sirloin in a skillet over medium heat. Drain off the excess fat.

Transfer the cooked sirloin to a crock pot. Stir in the canned tomatoes, tomato sauce, beans (all undrained), onion, chili powder, mustard, salt, and bay leaf.

Cook for 4 hours in the crock pot on high, stirring occasionally.

Reduce the heat to low and continue cooking another 2 hours. Serve the chili with grated cheese or sour cream topping.

Yield: 6 to 12 servings

Suggested beverage: Bell's Lager, Bell's Brewery, Galesburg, Michigan

Sour Cream Topping

1 cup sour cream

⅓ cup mild salsa

2 tablespoons mayonnaise

1 teaspoon chili powder

½ teaspoon onion powder

½ teaspoon curry powder

¼ teaspoon cayenne pepper

1 tablespoon lemon juice

1 teaspoon Dijon mustard

Combine the ingredients in a mixing bowl. Stir until smooth and creamy. Cover and refrigerate. Serve as a generous dollop over chili.

Yield: 1½ cups

White Chili

2 tablespoons extra-virgin olive oil

1 pound boneless, skinless chicken breast

2 red bell peppers, seeded and diced

1 medium onion, chopped

3 cloves garlic, minced

1 (4-ounce) can of chopped green chilies, drained

1 tablespoon chili powder

1 teaspoon ground cumin

1 teaspoon dried oregano

2 cups chicken broth

2 cups heavy cream

2 cups Great Northern Beans, fully cooked

½ cup chopped fresh cilantro

½ cup crumbled aged farmhouse Cheddar cheese

Sauté the chicken breast in 1 tablespoon of oil in a stock pot over medium heat until the chicken is browned, 2 to 3 minutes per side. Remove the chicken from the pot and cut it into ½-inch cubes. Set the chicken aside.

Add the remaining oil and sauté the peppers, onion, and garlic until the garlic just begins to brown. Add the green chilies, chili powder, cumin, and oregano and continue stirring for another 1 to 2 minutes. Add the broth and cream. Bring to a boil while stirring. Lower the heat and stir in the chicken and beans. Cover and simmer for 20 minutes.

Stir in the cilantro. Ladle the chili into individual bowls and top with crumbled Cheddar.

Yield: 6 to 12 servings

Bay Scallop Chowder

2 leeks

6 tablespoons (¾ stick) unsalted butter

1 stalk celery, diced

2 medium onions, diced

1½ pounds potatoes, cut into ¾-inch cubes

1 tablespoon salt

1 quart chicken broth

1 pound bay scallops

2 cups heavy whipping cream

1 tablespoon chopped parsley plus additional for garnish

Salt and freshly ground pepper

Cut off and discard the greens. Dice the white part of the leeks. Melt the butter in a stock pot over medium heat. Sauté the leeks, celery, and onions until the onions are translucent.

Add the potatoes, salt, and chicken broth. Bring to a boil, stirring often and scraping the pan. Lower the heat and simmer for 30 minutes.

Add the scallops and continue to simmer while heating the cream.

Heat the whipping cream to a boil in another saucepan, stirring continuously.

Stir the hot cream into the chowder. Add the parsley and continue to simmer until the chowder thickens.

Serve in individual bowls, adding freshly ground pepper and a pinch of parsley.

Yield: 4 to 8 servings

Suggested wine: Sauvignon Blanc, Honig, Napa Valley, California

New England Clam Chowder

While Manhattan chowder is tomato-based, New England chowder is cream-based. Although chowders may include any mix of fish, shellfish, and vegetables, classic New England chowder is thick and creamy, with a slightly sweet aroma and plenty of savory clams, bacon, and potatoes. Slowly simmer this soup until the clams are tender.

4 thick slices smoked bacon
6 tablespoons (¾ stick) unsalted butter
1 small clove garlic, chopped
1 medium onion, diced
3 celery stalks, diced
⅓ cup all-purpose flour
4 cups heavy cream
½ cup half and half
1½ cups frozen chopped clams, thawed
2 ounces concentrated clam broth base
1¼ cups clam juice
1 teaspoon ground white pepper
1 teaspoon fresh marjoram
2 teaspoons chopped fresh basil
1 teaspoon dried oregano leaf
½ teaspoon dried thyme leaf
¼ pound new potatoes, diced
2 bay leaves
Fresh chopped dill
Fresh chopped parsley

Fry the bacon in a stock pot over medium heat until crisp. Drain it on paper towels.

Return the pot to the heat and add the butter. Sauté the garlic, onions, and celery until soft. Add the flour and stir until it becomes foamy.

Add the heavy cream and the half and half in a slow, continuous stream, stirring the mixture. Add the clams, clam concentrate, and juice while continuing to stir. When the mixture begins to boil, lower the heat. Stir in the pepper, marjoram, basil, oregano, and thyme.

Chop the bacon and add it to the chowder. Add the potatoes and the bay leaves.

Cover and cook for 30 minutes over low heat, stirring occasionally. Before serving, remove the bay leaves. Add pinches of dill and parsley to each serving.

Yield: 2 to 4 servings

Suggested wine: Fumé Blanc, Sonoma County, The Vineyards of Chateau St. Jean, Sonoma, California

Corn Chowder

6 thick slices bacon

2 tablespoons extra-virgin olive oil

1 cup chopped red onion

1 cup chopped leek

¾ cup chopped celery

4 cups chicken broth

3 cups heavy cream

4 cups fresh or frozen sweet corn

1 teaspoon fennel seed

1½ pounds red potatoes, unpeeled and cut into ½-inch cubes

½ cup mixed dried mushrooms

2 tablespoons dry sherry

1 teaspoon fresh thyme leaves

Fresh parsley for garnish

Freshly ground pepper

Fry the bacon in a stock pot over medium heat until crisp. Drain it on paper towels, then chop it.

Add the olive oil, onion, leek, and celery. Sauté until soft. Add the chicken broth and cream and continue stirring while the mixture comes to a boil.

Lower the heat and stir in the corn, fennel, potatoes, mushrooms, sherry, thyme, and chopped bacon. Cover and simmer, stirring occasionally, until the soup thickens, about 40 minutes.

Serve garnished with parsley and freshly ground pepper.

Yield: 4 to 8 servings

New England
Fall Festival

Bay Scallop Chowder   68
Sauvignon Blanc, Honig Vineyard and Winery,
Napa Valley, California

Pear and Stilton Salad   86
Riesling, Dr. Pauly Bergweiler, Bernkasteler Badstube
Kabinett, Germany

Stuffed Pork Tenderloin with Apricot Sauce   190
The Footbolt Shiraz, d'Arenberg, McLaren Vale, Australia

Roasted Fingerling Potatoes   118

Mixed Grilled Vegetables   126

Sauerkraut-Stuffed Apples   132

Pumpkin Cupcakes   232

Salads

I PREFER to make my own salad dressing. In the past I experimented with different recipes, and the result was always too acidic, too messy, or just too much waste. A simple oil and vinegar mix is easy. I always use a good, salad-friendly extra-virgin olive oil and a European vinegar, which has the higher acid content necessary for that extra boost. If it's too strong, I can always add water to dilute it. I also use a lot of sea salt and coarse pepper. In the end, if I need to rely on something that can't go wrong, I use my favorite combination of lemon olive oil and lemon vinegar. Simplicity is a good rule here, because a few high-quality ingredients truly epitomize the old saying that less is more.

Ribeye Steak and Potato Salad

This recipe is a perfect solution for grilled steak or smoked meat left over from last weekend's cookout. You can make the dressing in advance and re-frigerate it—it will keep for weeks until you're ready to enjoy it.

DRESSING:

> 2 cloves garlic, minced
>
> 1½ cups basil leaves
>
> 1 tablespoon Dijon mustard
>
> ½ cup extra-virgin olive oil
>
> 2 tablespoons white wine vinegar
>
> 1 teaspoon sea salt

SALAD:

> ¾ pound fingerling potatoes
>
> 1 pound boneless ribeye steak, trimmed
>
> 1 tablespoon crushed coriander seeds
>
> 1 teaspoon freshly ground pepper plus additional to taste
>
> ¾ cup halved grape tomatoes
>
> Pinch of sea salt
>
> 4 cups mixed salad greens
>
> ½ cup arugula
>
> 2 tablespoons grated Parmigiano-Reggiano cheese

Boil the potatoes in a saucepan over high heat until tender, about 10 minutes. Drain the potatoes and set them aside to cool.

Grill the steak over direct heat, 3 to 4 minutes per side for rare. Remove the steak from the grill and set it aside to cool.

Put the dressing ingredients in a blender or food processor and process un-til well mixed.

Slice the steak across the grain into thin strips. Cut the potatoes into ¾-inch pieces.

Toss the steak, potatoes, coriander, pepper, tomatoes, salt, and half of the dressing in a mixing bowl. Add the salad greens, arugula, and the remaining dress-ing and toss again.

Sprinkle a light coating of grated cheese and freshly ground pepper on each serving.

Yield: 4 servings

Suggested wine: Pinot Noir, Rex Hill, Willamette Valley, Oregon

Classic Chicken Salad

1 cup sour cream

⅔ cup mayonnaise

½ cup shredded white Cheddar cheese

1½ cups cooked boneless, skinless chicken breast, cut into ¾ inch pieces

1 (9-ounce) can pineapple tidbits, drained

1 cup chopped walnuts

½ cup sliced celery

Combine the sour cream, mayonnaise, and cheese in a mixing bowl.

Blend the chicken, pineapple, walnuts, and celery in a large mixing bowl. Add the mayonnaise mixture and stir until well blended.

Yield: 4 to 6 servings

Suggested wine: Chardonnay, Chateau Ste. Michelle, Columbia Valley, Washington

Chicken and Broccoli Salad

1 (10-ounce) jar mango chutney

½ cup mayonnaise

¼ teaspoon red pepper flakes

2 cloves garlic, minced

4 cups water

¼ cup soy sauce

2 pounds boneless, skinless chicken breast

2 cups broccoli florets

4 scallions with stems, chopped

1 red bell pepper, seeded and chopped

1 cup dried tart cherries

¼ cup slivered almonds

Combine the chutney, mayonnaise, pepper flakes, and garlic in a mixing bowl. Stir to form a chunky dressing. Cover and refrigerate.

Bring the water and soy sauce to a boil in a saucepan over high heat. Poach the chicken until it is white throughout, about 15 minutes. Slice it into ¾-inch cubes.

Toss the chicken, broccoli, scallions, bell pepper, cherries, and dressing in a mixing bowl. Cover the bowl with plastic wrap and refrigerate 1 hour.

Serve with almonds sprinkled on top.

Yield: 6 to 8 servings

Suggested wine: Riesling Kabinett, Hexamer, Nahe, Germany

Poached Chicken and Three Bean Salad

2 cups chicken stock

2 pounds boneless, skinless chicken breast

1 cup canned red kidney beans, rinsed and drained

1 cup canned white kidney (cannellini) beans, rinsed and drained

1 cup flageolets (French kidney beans), rinsed and drained

1 cup whole grape tomatoes

½ green bell pepper, seeded and thinly sliced

½ yellow bell pepper, seeded and thinly sliced

2 tablespoons balsamic vinegar

2 tablespoons extra-virgin olive oil

2 scallions with tops, chopped

Kosher salt and freshly ground pepper

Bring the broth to a boil in a saucepan over high heat. Lower the heat, add the chicken and poach, turning once, until the meat becomes white throughout, about 10 minutes. Cut into ½-inch cubes.

Stir together the beans, tomatoes, peppers, vinegar, oil, scallions, and chicken. Season with salt and freshly ground pepper to taste.

Yield: 6 to 8 servings

Suggested wine: Pinot Noir, Mark West, Sonoma County, California

Ginger Chicken and Wild Rice Salad

1 cup wild rice
1 cup dried cherries
1 cup pecan halves
1 cut-up roasted chicken (page 154) or cooked rotisserie chicken
2 teaspoons candied ginger
1 bunch parsley, stemmed and chopped
1 cup diced celery
1 cup mix diced red, orange, and yellow bell pepper
Bottled vinaigrette
Mixed salad greens or radicchio
1 large fennel bulb, rinsed, trimmed, and finely sliced

Preheat the oven to 300 degrees.

Cook the wild rice according to the instructions on the package. Let the rice cool.

Put the cherries in a small bowl and cover them with hot water. Let soak for 20 minutes, then drain.

Spread the pecans on a baking sheet. Bake until their surface becomes well oiled, 8 to 10 minutes.

Remove and discard the skin from the chicken. Pull the meat from the bones and put it in a large mixing bowl. Add the rice, candied ginger, parsley, celery, peppers, pecans, drained cherries, and fennel and toss.

Add your favorite bottled vinaigrette and toss again to bind the dressing and salad. Serve over a bed of mixed greens or radicchio leaves.

Yield: 4 to 6 servings

Suggested wine: Gewurztraminer, Trimbach, Alsace, France

Grilled Shrimp and Asparagus Salad

½ pound medium shrimp, peeled and deveined

1 pound asparagus

3 tablespoons extra-virgin olive oil

Kosher salt and freshly ground pepper

1 tablespoon buttermilk

1 tablespoon honey mustard

1 teaspoon rice wine vinegar

1 (11-ounce) can mandarin oranges, juice reserved or 1 fresh orange,
   peeled and sectioned

½ teaspoon celery seed

½ pound jicama, peeled and sliced into thin strips

¼ medium red onion, thinly sliced

1 bunch romaine lettuce leaves, rinsed and trimmed

¼ cup blue cheese, crumbled

Prepare a fire for grilling.

Skewer the shrimp. Brush the shrimp and asparagus with olive oil and season with salt and pepper.

Grill the shrimp and asparagus over high, direct heat until the asparagus is tender, 5 to 7 minutes, turning once. Remove the shrimp and asparagus from the grill. Cut the asparagus into 2-inch pieces.

Stir together the buttermilk, mustard, vinegar, orange juice, and celery seed in a large mixing bowl.

Add the asparagus, shrimp, jicama, oranges, and red onion slices and toss.

Serve over romaine lettuce with freshly ground pepper and blue cheese sprinkled on top.

Yield: 16 to 20 servings

Suggested wine: Sauvignon Blanc, St. Supéry, Napa Valley, California

Caesar Salad

Supposedly, Caesar Cardini created his namesake salad in the 1920s in Tijuana, where wealthy Californians wintered to escape Prohibition and enjoy gambling. Caesar Salad makes an elegant presentation when prepared at the table in a large wooden bowl. Anchovies are optional, but to keep the flavor of Cardini's original vision, at least use anchovy juice. For an entrée salad, add grilled chicken breast strips or shrimp on top of each serving.

⅔ cup extra-virgin olive oil

2 cloves garlic, crushed

12 (¼-inch thick) slices of French baguette

¼ cup lemon juice

1 tablespoon red wine vinegar

½ teaspoon Worcestershire sauce

1 egg

½ cup grated Parmigiano-Reggiano cheese

Kosher salt and freshly ground pepper

2 heads romaine lettuce, rinsed, trimmed, and patted dry

2 anchovies, optional

To make the croutons, heat ⅓ cup olive oil in a skillet over medium heat. Sauté the garlic until browned, about 5 minutes. Discard the garlic.

Using tongs, toast the slices of bread in the oil for about 15 seconds per side. Set the croutons aside.

Bring to a boil in a small saucepan enough water to cover the egg. Remove the pan from the heat. Coddle the egg by letting it sit in the hot water, off heat, for 10 minutes.

Whisk together the lemon juice, vinegar, Worcestershire, and egg in a large salad bowl until the mixture is smooth and slightly foamy. Add the oil, cheese, salt, and pepper, stirring vigorously. Add the croutons and lettuce and toss well to coat the lettuce and distribute the croutons.

Add the anchovies and toss again.

Yield: 4 to 6 servings

Suggested wine: Prosecco, Zardetto Brut, Conegliano, Italy

Creamy Sweet and Sour Slaw

1 cup mayonnaise

½ cup sour cream

¼ cup freshly squeezed orange juice

2 tablespoons cider vinegar

2 large basil leaves, minced

2 tart baking apples, cored and thinly sliced

1 pound of jicama, peeled and thinly sliced

2 carrots, thinly sliced

½ small head cabbage, shredded

Kosher salt and freshly ground pepper

Whisk the mayonnaise, sour cream, orange juice, and vinegar in a large mixing bowl.

Add the basil, apples, jicama, carrots, and cabbage and toss until well mixed. Add salt and pepper to taste.

Yield: 8 servings

Tidewater Cabbage Slaw

1 ¼ cups mayonnaise
¼ cup barbecue sauce
¼ cup sugar
1 teaspoon celery seed
½ teaspoon kosher salt
1 teaspoon freshly ground pepper
2 carrots, finely grated
1 head green cabbage, finely shredded
Kosher salt and freshly ground pepper

Whisk the mayonnaise, barbecue sauce, sugar, celery seed, salt, and pepper in a large mixing bowl until smooth. Mix in the carrot. Add the cabbage and toss until the dressing is evenly distributed. Add salt and pepper to taste. Cover and refrigerate until ready to serve.

Yield: 8 to 12 servings

Cranberry and Cream Salad

Cranberries are only harvested once a year, so we only sell this salad in our deli case during the week of Thanksgiving, when they're fresh—but we sell a lot of it! In the fall, pick up an extra bag or two of cranberries and freeze them so you can enjoy this recipe with turkey all year round.

1 pound fresh cranberries, rinsed
1 cup red seedless grapes
1 cup unpeeled apples, cored and chopped
1 cup pineapple chunks, drained
½ cup chopped pecans
1 cup heavy whipping cream
1 cup sugar

Coarsely chop the cranberries in a food processor. Drain them in a colander.

Combine the cranberries, grapes, apples, pineapple, and pecans in a large bowl and mix well.

Whip the heavy cream at high speed with an electric mixer until it holds stiff peaks. Fold in the sugar.

Fold the sweetened whipped cream into the fruit. Serve chilled.

Yield: 4 to 6 servings

Fresh Fig Salad

⅓ cup balsamic vinegar

1 teaspoon lemon juice

¾ cup extra-virgin olive oil

Kosher salt and freshly ground pepper

18 fresh ripe figs

½ cup crumbled Italian Gorgonzola cheese

⅓ cup roasted and chopped hazelnuts

Mixed salad greens

Whisk the vinegar and lemon juice in a bowl. Add the olive oil in a slow, steady stream, whisking continuously. Add salt and pepper to taste.

Rinse the figs and slice them in half from the top downward.

Arrange the figs on serving plates over a bed of mixed greens and sprinkle the Gorgonzola and nuts over them. Drizzle dressing over the figs.

Yield: 6 servings

Suggested wine: Syrah, Cline Cellars, Sonoma, California

Pear and Stilton Salad

This fruit salad is perfect with aged balsamic vinegar. Authentic balsamic vinegar is only made in Italy's Modena region, according to specific standards of quality. White Trebbiano grapes are cooked down to a thick juice and aged in wooden barrels for up to a hundred years. The aging reduces the acidity, increases the viscosity, and perfects the sweetness of the vinegar.

> 2 ripe pears, rinsed and cored
> 4 tablespoons (½ stick) unsalted butter
> 2 cups mixed lettuce greens
> ¼ cup crumbled Stilton cheese
> ½ cup aged balsamic vinegar
> ¼ cup extra-virgin olive oil
> Freshly ground pepper

Cut each pear into 8 long wedges.

Melt the butter and sauté the pears in a saucepan over medium heat for 5 minutes, turning them once. Remove the pan from the heat.

Place an even bed of salad greens on four plates. Sprinkle the cheese evenly over the greens. Place the pears on top of the cheese.

Add the balsamic vinegar and olive oil to the pan in which the pears were cooked. Stir the mixture for 2 to 3 minutes over medium heat.

Drizzle the warm sauce over the salad and sprinkle with freshly ground pepper.

Yield: 4 servings

Suggested wine: Riesling, Dr. Pauly Bergweiler, Bernkasteler Badstube Kabinett, Germany

Orzo Pasta Salad

Don't let the number of ingredients scare you. Besides boiling the pasta, all you need to do for this recipe is toss together the prepped ingredients. The dressing can be made in advance and will keep refrigerated for several weeks. Be sure to wait until just before serving to mix in the sunflower seeds and carrots.

DRESSING:

   1 teaspoon salt

   ½ cup corn oil

   ¼ cup plus 2 tablespoons sesame oil

   ½ cup rice vinegar

   2 tablespoons rice wine or dry sherry

   1 teaspoon grated orange peel

   1 teaspoon soy sauce

   3 tablespoons thinly sliced scallions

   1½ teaspoons minced ginger

   ½ teaspoon minced garlic

   ¼ teaspoon red pepper flakes

   1 teaspoon freshly ground pepper

   1 tablespoon sugar

   3 tablespoons minced fresh coriander or parsley

SALAD:

   1 pound orzo pasta

   1 tablespoon dark sesame oil

   2 cups white raisins

   3 cups carrots, sliced into thin strips

   1 cup pine nuts, toasted

Combine all the dressing ingredients in a blender and mix well.

Bring a large pot of water to a boil. Stir in a tablespoon of salt and the orzo. Boil until al dente. Drain the pasta.

Toss the pasta, sesame oil, raisins, carrots, and pine nuts together in a mixing bowl. Pour the salad dressing over the orzo salad and toss again.

Yield: 6 to 8 servings

Suggested wine: Gewürztraminer, Chateau Ste. Michelle, Columbia Valley, Washington

Tortellini Salad with Red Wine Dressing

1 pound cheese tortellini pasta

¼ pound San Danielle or Parma prosciutto, thinly sliced and cut into
    1-inch pieces

½ seedless cucumber, peeled, quartered lengthwise, and sliced into
    1-inch pieces

1 yellow bell pepper, cut into strips lengthwise and sliced into 1-inch pieces

1 red bell pepper, cut into strips lengthwise and sliced into 1-inch pieces

¼ red onion, diced

20 grape tomatoes, cut in half

20 Kalamata olives, cut in half

1 cup crumbled feta cheese

½ cup extra-virgin olive oil

⅓ cup red wine vinegar

1 tablespoon kosher salt

Fresh dill

Bring a large pot of water to a boil. Stir in a tablespoon of salt and the pasta. Stir and cook according to the package directions. Drain the pasta.

Blend the prosciutto, cucumber, yellow and red peppers, onion, tomatoes, olives, and feta cheese in a large bowl.

Add the pasta, olive oil, and kosher salt and toss.

Let the salad sit for a few minutes. Add the red wine vinegar, kosher salt, and dill and toss the salad again.

Cover and refrigerate for one hour before serving.

Yield: 6 to 8 servings

Suggested wine: Soave Classico, Inama, Verona, Italy

Bow Tie Salad with Sun-Dried Tomatoes

SALAD:

> 1 tablespoon kosher salt
>
> 1 pound bow tie (farfalle) pasta
>
> 3 scallions, finely chopped
>
> 1½ ounces. sun-dried tomatoes, cut into strips
>
> 1 bunch fresh spinach, trimmed and shredded
>
> ¼ pound prosciutto, sliced into thin strips
>
> ⅓ cup toasted pine nuts
>
> 1 tablespoon chopped fresh oregano
>
> ¼ cup flaked Parmigiano-Reggiano cheese

DRESSING:

> ¼ cup extra-virgin olive oil
>
> 1 teaspoon red pepper flakes
>
> 1 clove garlic, crushed
>
> ½ teaspoon kosher salt
>
> ½ teaspoon freshly ground pepper

Bring a large pot of water to a boil. Stir in the salt and the pasta. Boil until al dente. Drain the pasta.

Put the pasta in a large salad bowl. Add the scallions, tomato, spinach, prosciutto, pine nuts, and oregano and toss.

For the dressing, whisk the oil, pepper flakes, garlic, salt, and pepper in a small bowl. Pour the dressing over the pasta. Toss well and garnish with Parmigiano-Reggiano cheese.

Yield: 6 to 8 servings

Suggested wine: Naia Verdejo, Bodegas Naia, Rueda, Spain

Creamy Chicken and Pasta Salad

½ pound rotini or fusilli pasta

½ pound fresh cream cheese

¾ cup sour cream

¼ cup half and half

1 tablespoon chopped fresh basil

1 teaspoon finely chopped fresh chives

2 cups poached chicken breast, cut into ¾-inch cubes

1 cup chopped celery

¼ cup chopped (½-inch pieces) red bell pepper

¼ cup chopped (½-inch pieces) orange bell pepper

Salt and freshly ground pepper

Bring a large pot of water to a boil. Stir in a tablespoon of salt and the pasta. Boil the pasta until al dente. Drain the pasta and let it cool.

Stir together the cream cheese, sour cream, half and half, basil, and chives in a mixing bowl until well blended.

Stir together the cooled pasta, chicken, celery, and peppers in a serving bowl.

Add the cream mixture to the pasta and toss lightly. Season to taste with salt and freshly ground pepper.

Serve immediately, or cover and refrigerate. To refresh the salad after refrigerating, stir in a little half and half.

Yield: 6 to 8 servings

Suggested wine: White Bordeaux, Château Lamothe de Haux, Bordeaux, France

Luncheon with Friends

White Asparagus Soup   62

Curried Chicken Salad Pitas   26

Orzo Pasta Salad   87
Gewürztraminer, Chateau Ste. Michelle,
Columbia Valley, Washington

Triple Berry Mini Tarts   222

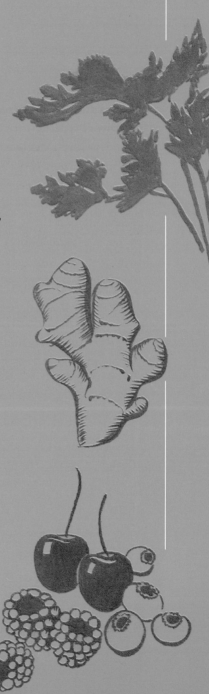

Herbed Shrimp and Pasta Salad

A balance of herbs gives this salad a delicate but distinctive touch. You can serve this salad as a first course or as a healthy stand-alone entrée. Feel free to substitute chunks of grilled chicken or roast turkey breast.

½ cup extra-virgin olive oil
¼ cup lemon juice
¼ cup chopped parsley
½ teaspoon chopped tarragon
1 teaspoon chopped rosemary
½ teaspoon chopped oregano
½ teaspoon chopped basil
¼ teaspoon salt
½ teaspoon freshly ground pepper
1 pound rotini pasta
1 tablespoons pickling spices
1 bottle dark ale
1 pound medium shrimp, peeled and deveined

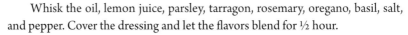

Whisk the oil, lemon juice, parsley, tarragon, rosemary, oregano, basil, salt, and pepper. Cover the dressing and let the flavors blend for ½ hour.

Bring a large pot of water to a boil. Stir in a tablespoon of salt and the pasta. Boil until al dente. Drain the pasta, toss it with a little olive oil, and set it aside to cool.

Heat the pickling spices, ale, and 2 cups of water in a large saucepan over medium-high heat. When the water begins to boil, add the shrimp and gently stir while they cook. Adjust the heat so the water does not boil over. The shrimp will be done when they have turned a light orange. Do not overcook them. Drain and rinse the shrimp immediately to stop the cooking process.

To serve, toss together the pasta, shrimp, and dressing.

Yield: 6 to 8 servings

Suggested wine: Pomelo Sauvignon Blanc, Mason Cellars, Oakville, California

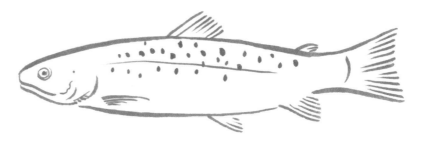

Grilled Salmon Pasta Salad

½ pound fusilli pasta

2 tablespoons extra-virgin olive oil

1 cup mayonnaise

2 tablespoons lemon juice

1 tablespoon capers

¾ cup chopped roasted red peppers

½ small red onion, chopped

½ teaspoon sea salt plus additional

1 teaspoon freshly ground pepper plus additional

1 pound boneless salmon fillet

2 tablespoons chopped fresh parsley

1 hard boiled egg, chopped

Bring a large pot of water to a boil. Stir in a tablespoon of salt and the pasta. Boil until al dente. Drain the pasta and return it to the pot. Add 1 tablespoon of the olive oil and toss until the pasta is coated. Set aside to cool.

Stir together the mayonnaise, lemon juice, capers, peppers, onion, egg, ½ teaspoon sea salt, and 1 teaspoon pepper in a small mixing bowl. Put the bowl in the refrigerator while grilling the salmon.

Brush the salmon with the remaining 1 tablespoon of olive oil and sprinkle it with freshly ground pepper and sea salt. Grill the salmon skin side up on a hot grate over direct heat. After 3 minutes, use a spatula to loosen the salmon from the grate and rotate it a quarter turn. After 3 more minutes, turn the salmon skin side down. Grill the salmon until it flakes easily when a fork is inserted, another 4 to 6 minutes.

Remove the salmon from the grill and let it sit for 5 minutes on a cutting board. Peel away the skin and trim any fat next to the skin. Slice the salmon into ¾-inch cubes.

Gently fold the salmon, the mayonnaise mixture, and the parsley into the pasta until all the ingredients are well mixed.

Yield: 12 to 14 servings

Suggested wine: Unoaked Chardonnay, Mackenzie Vineyards, Sonoma, California

Pasta Salad with Turkey Breast

This is a tasty use for leftover turkey on that sleepy Saturday after Thanksgiving. For a convenient lunch, make it a day or two in advance and cover it tightly. It's perfect as a pasta salad but also works well in a sandwich with a little lettuce. If you don't already have turkey in the refrigerator, choose a whole-muscle breast of turkey from your deli and have it sliced half- to three-quarter-inch thick. This recipe also works well with chicken breast or even grilled shrimp.

1 cup rotini pasta

½ cup slivered almonds, toasted

2 cups fresh sugar snap peas, trimmed

½ cup mayonnaise

½ cup sour cream

1 teaspoon soy sauce

½ teaspoon freshly ground pepper

2 cups cubed turkey breast

½ cup chopped scallions

½ cup sliced water chestnut, rinsed and drained

Romaine lettuce leaves, rinsed and trimmed

½ teaspoon chopped ginger

Preheat the oven to 350 degrees.

Bring a large pot of water to a boil. Stir in a tablespoon of salt and the pasta. Boil until al dente. Reserve ½ cup of pasta water and drain the pasta. Set the pasta aside.

Spread the almonds on a baking sheet and toast them in the oven until their oil comes to the surface and they begin to brown. Be careful not to let them burn. Remove them from the oven and set aside to cool.

Bring a saucepan of water to a boil. Add the snap peas and cover the pan. Blanch the peas in the boiling water for 2 minutes. Drain the peas into a colander. Rinse the peas thoroughly in cold water to rapidly cool them down.

Combine the mayonnaise, sour cream, soy sauce, pepper, and ginger in a small mixing bowl.

Toss the pasta, almonds, peas, turkey, scallions, and chestnuts in a large bowl until the ingredients are well mixed. Stir in the mayonnaise mixture. Cover the bowl with plastic wrap and put the salad in the refrigerator for 3 hours.

To serve, spoon the pasta salad onto a serving dish lined with lettuce leaves.

Yield: 6 to 8 servings

Pasta

MY FAVORITE pasta dish is mac and cheese, for the eternal child in all of us. Over the years I've tweaked the recipe to change it from a side dish to a hearty meal. I use mini penne, mascarpone, cream cheese, Parmigiano-Reggiano cheese, milk, spinach, pinched sausage, and farmer's bread soaked in milk over the top. Due to the richness of the dish, it goes well with a light red wine such as Pinot Noir.

The important thing about pasta, aside from quality, is presentation. In our "chef's case," or deli, we used to put the pasta in a big bowl, with the garnishes on the side in another. Now we present our pasta in little stacks twirled into nests with eye-catching garnishes on the side. The idea of selling attractive individual servings with the finest quality pastas caught on, and now we can't make them fast enough.

West Point Mac and Cheese

For our take on this American classic, we use a rich blend of four cheeses: cream cheese, sweet mascarpone, tangy blue Gorgonzola, and aged Parmigiano-Reggiano.

1 pound penne pasta

¾ pound bulk sausage

1 generous cup of firm French baguette, cut into 1-inch cubes

1½ cups whole milk

2 tablespoons unsalted butter

3 cloves garlic, pressed

1 cup grated Parmigiano-Reggiano cheese

½ pound fresh cream cheese, softened

½ pound mascarpone cheese

¼ pound Gorgonzola cheese

1 teaspoon kosher salt

1 teaspoon freshly cracked peppercorns

¼ teaspoon ground nutmeg

1 pound fresh spinach, rinsed well

Preheat the oven to 400 degrees.

Bring a large pot of water to a boil. Stir in a tablespoon of salt and the pasta. Boil until al dente. Drain the pasta and set it aside.

Brown the sausage in a skillet over medium heat. Drain the sausage and set it aside.

Put the bread in a mixing bowl and moisten it with ½ cup of the milk.

Melt the butter in a 3-quart saucepan over medium heat. Sauté the garlic until just tender. Add the remaining cup of milk and stir the mixture until heated.

Set the heat on medium-low and gradually stir in ½ cup of the Parmigiano-Reggiano cheese, the cream cheese, the mascarpone, and the Gorgonzola until melted. Add the salt, cracked pepper, and nutmeg and stir until smooth and creamy.

Remove the mixture from the heat and stir in the spinach, cooked pasta, and sausage. Spoon the mixture into a lightly greased 9 by 13-inch baking dish.

Bake for 7 minutes. Remove the dish from the oven and sprinkle the bread cubes and the remaining ½ cup of Parmigiano-Reggiano over the dish.

Lower the oven temperature to 350 degrees and bake for an additional 20 minutes. Finish under the broiler until golden brown on top.

Yield: 6 to 8 servings

Suggested wine: Riff Pinot Grigio, Alois Lageder, Venezie, Italy

Fettuccine Alfredo

For a more robust meal, you can add chicken breast, shrimp, or scallops to the Alfredo. Vegetables such as asparagus or broccoli florets also go well with this creamy sauce. Like whipped cream, Alfredo sauce can be frozen. For a quick, foolproof, but impressive dinner entrée, swirl pre-cooked toppings with a generous scoop of Alfredo in a skillet, and combine with freshly cooked pasta.

1 pint heavy whipping cream
1 teaspoon kosher salt
1 teaspoon freshly ground black pepper
2 tablespoons chopped fresh parsley
¼ cup grated pecorino Romano cheese
1 pound fettuccine pasta
¼ pound (1 stick) unsalted butter, melted
¼ cup grated Parmigiano-Reggiano cheese

Using an electric mixer, whip the heavy cream, salt, pepper, and parsley to form stiff peaks. Stir in the Romano cheese. Cover and refrigerate or freeze for later use.

Bring a large pot of water to a boil. Stir in a tablespoon of salt and the pasta. Boil until al dente. Drain the pasta.

Melt the butter in a large skillet over medium heat, stirring. Add the drained pasta to the skillet and stir to coat the pasta with butter. Spoon the Alfredo sauce into the skillet and continue to stir for 2 to 3 minutes.

Remove the pasta from the heat and spoon onto serving plates. If desired, place grilled chicken or shrimp over the pasta. Top with grated Parmigiano-Reggiano cheese.

Yield: 4 servings

Suggested wine: Salice Salentino, Taurino, Apulia, Italy

Baked Orecchiette with Cream Sauce

Pecorino Romano is a hard Italian cheese similar to Parmigiano (Parmesan), but with a slightly sharper flavor. Pecorino is made from sheep's milk while Parmigiano comes from cows. With either cheese, aging produces fuller flavors and more complex textures. When a recipe calls for adding Italian cheese during cooking, we prefer pecorino because it doesn't stick to the sides of the pan like Parmigiano.

½ pound orecchiette pasta

½ pound fresh ricotta cheese

½ cup flaked Parmigiano-Reggiano cheese

¼ cup sour cream at room temperature

2 cups canned chicken stock

3 cloves garlic, minced

4 fresh basil leaves, chopped

¼ teaspoon salt

½ teaspoon red pepper flakes

1 pound fresh mozzarella, sliced ¼ inch thick

¼ cup grated pecorino Romano cheese

Preheat the oven to 350 degrees.

Bring a large pot of water to a boil. Stir in a tablespoon of salt and the pasta. Boil until al dente. Drain the pasta.

For the cheese sauce, blend the ricotta, Parmigiano-Reggiano, and sour cream in a large bowl. Whisk in the chicken stock, garlic, basil, salt, and pepper flakes. Add the pasta and gently stir until thoroughly mixed.

Spray or oil a baking dish and pour in half the pasta and half the cheese sauce. Cover the mixture with slices of fresh mozzarella. Sprinkle 2 tablespoons of Romano cheese over the mozzarella.

Pour the remaining pasta and cheese sauce into the baking dish. Add another layer of mozzarella and sprinkle with the remaining Romano.

Bake for 25 to 30 minutes. Fresh mozzarella doesn't brown like the low moisture variety used as pizza cheese, so the cheese will still be fairly white when you remove the dish from the oven.

Serve with additional Romano or Parmigiano-Reggiano, as desired.

Yield: 6 to 8 servings

Suggested wine: Sangiovese, Monte Antico, Tuscany, Italy

Avocado Basil Farfalle

1 pound farfalle or bow-tie pasta

½ cup pine nuts

6 slices peppered bacon

2 ripe avocados

3 tablespoons extra-virgin olive oil

3 cloves garlic, finely minced

12 sun-dried tomatoes in oil, drained

1 cup Peppadew sweet piquanté peppers

⅔ cup chopped fresh basil

¼ cup fresh lemon juice

¼ teaspoon coarse ground black pepper

¼ teaspoon salt

½ cup grated pecorino Romano cheese

Preheat the oven to 350 degrees.

Bring a large pot of water to a boil. Stir in a tablespoon of salt and the pasta. Boil the pasta until al dente. Drain the pasta well.

While the pasta is cooking, toast the pine nuts on a baking sheet until they are an oily golden brown, 5 to 7 minutes.

Fry the bacon in a large skillet on medium-high heat until crisp. Drain it on paper towels and chop it into small pieces.

Cut the avocados in half and remove the seeds. Peel the avocados and coarsely chop them.

Pour 1 tablespoon of olive oil in a large pan and heat on medium-high. Sauté the garlic until tender.

Remove the pan from the heat and stir in the avocados, bacon, sun-dried tomatoes, toasted pine nuts, Peppadew peppers, basil, lemon juice, the remaining 2 tablespoons of olive oil, the black pepper, salt, and ¼ cup of the cheese. Add the hot pasta and stir gently until thoroughly mixed.

Transfer to a serving bowl and sprinkle with the remaining ¼ cup of cheese.

Yield: 4 servings

Suggested wine: Cetamura Chianti, Coltibuono, Tuscany, Italy

Walnut and Garlic Linguine

For this northern Italian dish, garlic and walnuts are sautéed in oil; the remaining ingredients are simply tossed with the cooked pasta. Our favorite variations include the addition of sautéed porcini mushrooms, thin strips of imported prosciutto, or a handful of capers. To crumble Italian Gorgonzola, use a fork and mash the cheese on a paper towel.

1 pound linguine

3 tablespoons olive oil

4 cloves garlic, minced

¾ cup chopped walnuts

¼ cup chopped parsley

¼ cup fresh basil, chopped

½ teaspoon salt

1 teaspoon freshly ground pepper

⅓ cup grated pecorino Romano cheese

½ cup crumbled Italian Gorgonzola cheese

⅓ cup grated Parmigiano-Reggiano cheese

Bring a large pot of water to a boil. Stir in a tablespoon of salt and the pasta. As the pasta begins to soften, work it into the pot to immerse it completely in the water. Boil the pasta until al dente. Drain the pasta well.

Heat the olive oil in a large skillet over medium heat. Add the garlic and walnuts and stir until the walnuts are lightly toasted, 5 to 6 minutes.

Add the hot pasta, parsley, basil, salt, pepper, Romano, and ¼ cup of the Gorgonzola cheese. Stir until thoroughly combined.

Put the pasta in a serving dish. Garnish with Parmigiano-Reggiano and the remaining ¼ cup of Gorgonzola cheese and serve immediately.

Yield: 4 servings

Suggested wine: Santa Cristina Sangiovese, Antinori, Tuscany, Italy

Penne with Spinach and Pine Nuts

Here's our tip for peeling tomatoes the easy way: submerge them in a bowl of boiling water. After a few minutes, you can slit the skin and it will slide right off.

⅓ cup olive oil

6 cloves fresh garlic, finely chopped

½ cup pine nuts

8–10 whole plum tomatoes, peeled and cored

2 (10-ounce) packages of frozen chopped spinach, thawed and drained

½ teaspoon garlic paste

1 cup chicken broth

1 teaspoon garlic powder

Salt and freshly ground pepper

1 pound penne rigate pasta

½ cup grated Parmigiano-Reggiano cheese

Shaved Asiago cheese for garnish

Heat the olive oil in a large skillet over medium heat. Sauté the garlic and pine nuts until they are light brown, about 5 minutes.

Add the tomatoes and raise the heat to medium-high. Allow the tomatoes to soften, then stir and press them with a fork until they have the consistency of a chunky sauce.

Lower the heat, cover, and continue to simmer for 15 to 20 minutes, stirring occasionally. Do not allow mixture to become dry.

Add the spinach, garlic paste, chicken broth, garlic powder, and salt and pepper to taste. Let simmer covered an additional 15 to 20 minutes, stirring occasionally. If the mixture gets too dry, add more chicken broth.

Bring a large pot of water to a boil. Stir in a tablespoon of salt and the pasta. Boil the pasta until al dente. Drain the pasta well.

Place the pasta in a deep serving platter. Fold the Parmigiano-Reggiano cheese into the sauce. Spoon the sauce over the pasta and garnish with shaved Asiago cheese.

Yield: 4 servings

Suggested wine: Merlot, Burgess, Napa Valley, California

Rigatoni with Rabe

Ordinary table salt is industrially mined and refined into almost pure sodium chloride, whereas sea salt is unrefined. It is made by a process of natural evaporation that allows it to retain trace minerals and organic components from the salt water, giving it a distinctive flavor that is different for each of the hundreds of varieties available. When buying sea salt, check the label to be sure the salt is completely natural and authentic.

> 1 tablespoon sea salt
>
> 1 bunch (about 1 pound) broccoli rabe, rinsed and cut into 2-inch pieces
>
> 2 tablespoons olive oil
>
> 3 garlic cloves, chopped
>
> 1 pound sweet Italian sausage, removed from casings
>
> 1 medium white onion, sliced thin
>
> 1 pound rigatoni pasta
>
> ½ teaspoon freshly ground pepper
>
> ⅓ cup grated Asiago cheese
>
> ¼ cup leaf parsley, rinsed and chopped
>
> 1 cup chicken broth

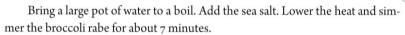

Bring a large pot of water to a boil. Add the sea salt. Lower the heat and simmer the broccoli rabe for about 7 minutes.

Heat the olive oil in a large skillet over low heat. Sauté the garlic until it softens. When the garlic just begins to brown, add the sausage and onion. Raise the heat to medium and sauté until the sausage is no longer pink, about 5 minutes, breaking up the sausage with a wooden spoon.

Remove the broccoli rabe from the water and stir it into the sausage mixture. Add the chicken broth. Simmer an additional 5 minutes, then remove from the heat.

Bring the water back to a boil and stir in the pasta. Boil the pasta until al dente. Drain the pasta well.

Add the pasta to the skillet. Add the pepper and stir to mix well.

Transfer to a serving dish. Sprinkle with Asiago cheese and chopped parsley.

Yield: 4 servings

Suggested wine: Rosso, Avignonesi, Montepulciano, Italy

Orzo with Mushrooms

This creamy garlic-and-cheese sauce is a perfect accompaniment for sea-food. We particularly recommend the meaty texture of grilled swordfish, sea bass, or flaky Alaskan halibut.

¾ cup orzo pasta
1 tablespoon unsalted butter
1 clove garlic, minced
½ cup white wine
1 teaspoon lemon
1 cup heavy cream
¼ teaspoon dried tarragon, crushed
1 tablespoon chopped chives
¼ cup dried porcini mushrooms
Kosher salt and freshly ground pepper
½ cup grated Italian fontina cheese
¼ cup slivered almonds
Zest of 1 lemon

Bring a large pot of water to a boil. Stir in a tablespoon of salt and the pasta. Boil until al dente. Reserve 2 cups of water, then drain the pasta.

Put the mushrooms in a small bowl and cover them with the reserved pasta water. Set aside.

Melt the butter in a saucepot over medium heat. Sauté the garlic until it just begins to brown. Add the white wine and lemon and cook, stirring, until reduced by half. Add the cream, tarragon, chives, and mushrooms and stir continuously, until the sauce thickens. Add salt and pepper to taste.

Lower the heat and add the cheese and almonds. Stir until smooth. Stir in the pasta.

Garnish each serving with lemon zest.

Yield: 4 servings

Eggplant Parmigiana

Substitute boneless skinless chicken breast for the eggplant to make Chicken Parmigiana.

1 large eggplant

Flour for dredging

2 eggs, beaten

Breadcrumbs for coating

Extra-virgin olive oil

1 (14-ounce) jar marinara sauce

1 pound fresh mozzarella, sliced

1½ cups freshly grated Parmigiano-Reggiano cheese

6 basil leaves, shredded

1 pound spaghetti

Preheat the oven to 375 degrees.

Peel the eggplant and cut it lengthwise into ¼-inch slices. Dredge the slices in the flour, then dip them in the egg, shaking off any excess. Coat the eggplant with breadcrumbs.

Pour the olive oil in a large skillet to a depth of ¼ inch and heat it over medium-high heat. Fry the eggplant strips until golden, about 2 minutes per side. Remove the eggplant from the skillet and drain it on paper towels.

Layer the eggplant, sauce, and cheese in a baking dish. Begin by covering the bottom of the dish with slices of fried eggplant, then cover the eggplant completely with marinara sauce. Scatter slices of mozzarella on top of the sauce and sprinkle Parmigiano-Reggiano and basil over them. Repeat with additional layers of eggplant, sauce, cheese, and basil until all the eggplant has been used, finishing with a layer of cheese and basil.

Bake until the cheese melts and is golden on top, about 20 minutes.

Bring a large pot of water to a boil. Stir in a tablespoon of salt and the pasta. As the pasta begins to soften, work it into the pot to immerse it completely in water. Boil the pasta until al dente. Drain the pasta well.

Serve the eggplant parmigiana over a portion of spaghetti with the remaining marinara sauce.

Yield: 4 to 6 servings

Suggested wine: Barbera, Montaribaldi, Piedmont, Italy

Fusilli with Chicken Sausage

If you want a slightly milder version of this sauce, you can substitute plum tomatoes for the Peppadew peppers.

3 tablespoons olive oil

1 pound fresh chicken sausage links

1 medium onion, finely chopped

2 cloves garlic, chopped

1½ cups sliced fresh mushrooms

8 to 10 Peppadew sweet piquanté peppers or 6 plum tomatoes, thinly sliced

½ cup pine nuts

½ cup dry white wine

1½ cups of prepared marinara sauce

¼ cup water

¼ teaspoon crumbled fresh rosemary

½ cup chopped fresh basil

Pinch of red pepper flakes

½ teaspoon salt

3 tablespoons chopped flat leaf parsley

1 pound fusilli pasta

¾ cup fresh ricotta cheese

Grated pecorino Romano cheese

Heat the olive oil in a medium skillet over medium-high heat. Sauté the chicken sausage until fully cooked, about 10 minutes. Set the sausage aside on paper towels until cool. Slice it into ¼-inch pieces.

In the same skillet, sauté the chopped onion and garlic over medium-high heat until soft, adding a little more oil, if needed. Add the mushrooms, Peppadew peppers, and pine nuts and sauté for about 5 minutes.

Add the wine, marinara sauce, water, rosemary, basil, pepper flakes, salt, and parsley and stir well. Lower the heat and let simmer.

Bring a large pot of water to a boil. Stir in a tablespoon of salt and the pasta. Boil the pasta until al dente. Drain the pasta well.

Toss the pasta, sauce, and sausage in a large serving bowl until well mixed. Add the ricotta and toss lightly.

Sprinkle pecorino Romano on top and garnish with fresh parsley.

Yield: 4 servings

Suggested wine: Rioja, Marqués de Cáceres, Rioja, Spain

Radiatore with Asparagus alla Carbonara

This recipe is a carbonara with a little bit of primavera (springtime). The dish itself uses raw eggs, which are slightly cooked by the heat from the piping hot pasta. Still, be sure to rinse the egg shells well and don't make this dish in advance or store it in the refrigerator.

4 large eggs

1 tablespoon plus ¼ teaspoon sea salt

½ cup freshly grated pecorino Romano cheese

2 tablespoons olive oil

1 medium yellow onion, halved and thinly sliced

¼ pound thin slices of pancetta, diced

1½ pounds pencil thin asparagus, rinsed and cut into 1 inch pieces

1 pound radiatore or penne pasta

Freshly ground pepper

½ cup freshly grated Parmigiano-Reggiano cheese

Crack the eggs into a small bowl and add ¼ teaspoon of the sea salt. Whisk the eggs until they foam. Stir in the pecorino Romano cheese. Keep the mixture cool in the refrigerator.

Heat 1 tablespoon olive oil in a large pan over medium heat. Sauté the onion and pancetta until softened. Add the asparagus and more oil, if needed, and continue to sauté the vegetables until the onions are browned on the edges.

Bring a large pot of water to a boil. Stir in the remaining 1 tablespoon of sea salt and the pasta. Boil the pasta until al dente.

Drain the pasta and return it to the pot while it is still very hot. Pour in the egg and cheese mixture and stir well. Add the asparagus, onion, pancetta, and pepper to taste and stir until well mixed.

Serve with Parmigiano-Reggiano cheese on the side.

Yield: 4 servings

Suggested wine: Pinot Gris, Adelsheim, Willamette Valley, Oregon

Sausage and Vegetable Ziti

2½ tablespoons extra-virgin olive oil

2 cloves fresh garlic, chopped

½ pound Italian link sausage, cut into ½ inch slices

2 cups broccoli florets

1 pound ziti pasta

Kernels from 2 large ears of fresh sweet corn

¼ pound of cherry tomatoes, halved

½ teaspoon kosher salt

½ teaspoon freshly ground pepper

¼ cup grated Parmigiano-Reggiano cheese plus extra for serving

Heat the oil in a large saucepan over medium heat. Sauté the garlic until it just begins to brown. Add the sausage and cook until the meat is browned, about 10 minutes. Reduce the heat to medium-low. Stir in the broccoli, cover, and cook an additional 5 minutes.

Bring a large pot of water to a boil. Stir in a tablespoon of salt and the pasta. Cook until al dente. Reserve ½ cup of water from the pasta and drain the pasta well.

Add the reserved pasta water to the sausage mixture. Stir in the corn, tomatoes, salt, and pepper and allow the mixture to boil for 1 minute.

Toss the pasta with the sausage mixture and the Parmigiano-Reggiano cheese in a large bowl until thoroughly mixed. Serve with additonal Parmigiano-Reggiano on the side.

Yield: 4 servings

Suggested wine: Zinfandel, Ravenswood, Sonoma, California

Linguine with Lobster Sauce

This recipe also works well with prawns, jumbo shrimp, or sea scallops.

4 (8-ounce) lobster tails
1 tablespoon chopped Italian parsley
1 (28-ounce) can Italian tomatoes, drained
1 garlic clove, minced
4 tablespoons (½ stick) melted unsalted butter
¼ cup fresh lemon juice
¼ cup dry white wine
1 pound linguine pasta
Extra-virgin olive oil
Salt and freshly ground pepper
¼ cup freshly grated Parmigiano-Reggiano cheese
Chopped fresh parsley

Preheat the oven to 350 degrees.

Peel away the lobster shells and remove the lobster meat. Cut the lobster meat into bite-size pieces and place them in a small bowl. Add the tomatoes, garlic, butter, lemon juice, and white wine.

Coat the bottom of a baking dish with a little olive oil. Put the lobster mixture in the baking dish. Bake on the middle rack of the oven for 12 to 15 minutes until the lobster is firm.

Bring a large pot of water to a boil. Stir in a tablespoon of salt and the pasta. As the pasta begins to soften, work it into the pot to immerse it completely in the water. Boil the pasta until al dente. Reserve ½ cup of the pasta water, then drain the pasta well.

Return the pasta to the cooking pot. Add the lobster mixture and reserved cooking water and cook on medium heat until the water is almost evaporated, about 5 minutes. Add olive oil, salt, and pepper to taste.

Spoon the linguine onto serving plates and sprinkle with Parmigiano-Reggiano cheese. Garnish with chopped parsley.

Yield: 4 servings

Suggested wine: Chardonnay, Saintsbury, Carneros, California

Scallops Italiano

3 tablespoons olive oil

1 pound sea scallops, rinsed and patted dry

3 tablespoons minced shallots

2 cups diced plum tomatoes

1 each red, yellow, and orange bell peppers, finely diced

3 tablespoons finely chopped basil

¼ cup dry white Italian wine

Salt and black pepper

1 pound bucatini pasta

Heat 2 tablespoons of the olive oil in a skillet over medium-high heat. Sauté the scallops for 5 minutes, turning once. Transfer the scallops to a plate.

Add another tablespoon of olive oil to the skillet and cook the shallots until soft. Add the tomatoes, peppers, and basil. Stir and cook until the peppers are soft.

Add the wine. Stir and simmer over low heat for 5 minutes. Add the cooked scallops and salt and pepper to taste.

Bring a large pot of water to a boil. Stir in a tablespoon of salt and the pasta. As the pasta begins to soften, work it into the pot to immerse it completely in the water. Boil the pasta until al dente. Drain the pasta well.

To serve, spoon the scallop mixture over the pasta.

Yield: 6 to 8 servings

Suggested wine: Barbera d'Alba, Corino, Piedmont, Italy

Wild Mushroom Couscous

Couscous, a granular pasta made from semolina flour, is eaten throughout the Mediterranean region. By far the most popular is North African couscous, which is small and yellow-brown in color. Israeli couscous is about the size of a pea and off-white. You can serve couscous like pasta, as a bed for meat, fish, shellfish, or vegetables.

2 cups chicken or vegetable stock

2 tablespoons olive oil

½ cup diced onion

½ cup diced scallions

1 pound of mixed mushrooms, such as shitake, oyster, and cremini

½ cup diced sun-dried tomatoes

2 cups couscous

Salt and freshly ground pepper

Bring the stock to a boil in a small pan and set it aside.

Heat the olive oil in a large skillet over medium heat. Sauté the onion, scallions, and mushrooms until the onions are soft. Stir in the tomatoes and couscous.

Pour in the stock, lower the heat, cover, and cook for 8 minutes.

Spoon the couscous into a serving bowl. Stir in salt and pepper to taste.

Yield: 4 servings

Spätzle

Serve these German dumplings as a side dish with melted butter or gravy, or add them to soup.

3 eggs
3 cups all-purpose flour
¼ teaspoon salt
1 cup milk

Fill a stockpot half full of water and bring it to a boil.

Meanwhile, beat the eggs in a mixing bowl until frothy.

Sift the flour and salt. Add the flour and milk alternately to the beaten eggs to make a smooth dough.

For noodles, hold a large-hole colander or slotted spoon over the water and push the dough through the holes.

For dumplings, drop teaspoon-sized portions of dough into the boiling water.

Gently stir the water to keep the dough from sticking. When the spätzle are done, they will float on top of the water. Quickly rinse them in cool water.

Yield: 4 to 6 servings

Traditional Italian Feast

Fresh Fig Salad   85
Syrah, Cline Cellars, Sonoma, California

Minestrone   56
Tempranillo, Marqués de Cáceres, Rioja, Spain

Walnut and Garlic Linguine   101
Santa Cristina Sangiovese, Antinori, Tuscany, Italy

Osso Bucco with Porcini Mushrooms   184
Mara Ripasso, Cesari, Veneto, Italy

Asparagus in Butter   123

Tiramisu Cheesecake   231

Fruits and Vegetables

I N THE 1940s, trucks lined up in front of the Beaver Street Farmers' Market every morning at 4 AM. Farmers came from small Ohio towns, driving their trucks or pickups hundreds of miles to sell produce and clucking chickens under long open-bay pavilions. Once they entered the gated area, they dropped their tailgates and began bargaining.

As a boy, I watched and learned as my father haggled over the price of wet Honey Rock melons, negotiated for the freshest corn—the kind that squirted when you pinched a kernel—and picked solid heads of iceberg lettuce. When farmers shouted out, "Just picked—red, ripe strawberries! Fifty-nine cents a quart!" he knew to inspect the bottom of the strawberry basket instead of the top, which was always showy.

I learned from my father at an early age that you have to be patient and careful when it comes to selecting the finest quality produce, whether it's for your business or the family dinner table.

Lake House Potato Bake

1 pound thickly sliced country bacon, sliced in 2-inch pieces

1 tablespoon sea salt

8 large white potatoes, peeled and cut 1-inch pieces

8 ounces sour cream

1½ pounds fresh cream cheese, softened

1 generous cup chopped scallions with greens

1 teaspoon freshly ground pepper

¼ pound (1 stick) butter, sliced into pats

½ pound shredded Swiss Gruyère cheese

½ cup chopped fresh parsley

Fry the bacon in a skillet over medium heat until crisp. Drain it on paper towels.

Fill a large pot one third full with water and add the sea salt. Add the potatoes and boil them until tender. Drain the potatoes.

Put the hot potatoes in a large mixing bowl and whip them with sour cream and softened cream cheese until smooth and creamy. Gently fold in the scallions and half the bacon. Add pepper to taste.

Spoon the mixture into a greased 9 by 13-inch baking dish and top with pats of butter, the cheese, and the remaining bacon.

Cover the baking dish and refrigerate overnight.

Preheat the oven to 325 degrees.

Cover and bake the potatoes for 15 minutes. Uncover and continue to bake an additional 20 minutes.

Top with chopped parsley. Serve as a side dish with steamed broccoli and grilled meats.

Yield: 12 to 14 servings

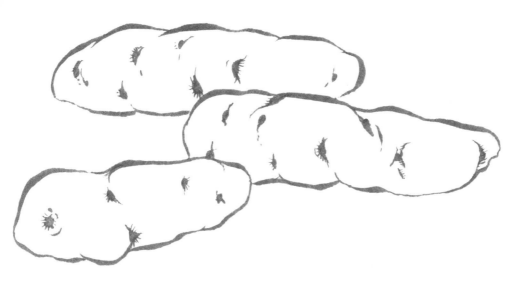

Roasted Fingerling Potatoes

Fingerling potatoes are a variety whose elongated tubers remain small when fully grown. As the name suggests, they are shaped like fingers. Don't confuse them with new potatoes, which are regular potatoes harvested before they reach maturity. There are many varieties of fingerlings but all will have that distinctive shape, thin skin, and the full, complex flavor of a mature potato.

> 1½ pounds fingerling potatoes, halved lengthwise
>
> 3 tablespoons extra-virgin olive oil
>
> 4 teaspoons fresh thyme leaves
>
> 4 garlic cloves, minced
>
> Kosher salt and freshly ground pepper
>
> Fresh chopped parsley

Preheat the oven to 400 degrees.

Mix the potatoes, oil, thyme, garlic, salt, and pepper.

Line a baking pan with parchment paper. Put the potatoes in the pan and roast them, uncovered, until tender, 20 to 25 minutes.

Sprinkle with parsley and serve.

Yield: 4 to 6 servings

Southern Red Garnets

6 to 8 Red Garnet sweet potatoes

¼ pound (1 stick) butter

1½ cups brown sugar

¼ teaspoon cinnamon

¼ teaspoon nutmeg

1 tablespoon all-purpose flour

¼ cup chopped pecans

¼ cup currants

Preheat the oven to 350 degrees.

Rinse, peel, and cut the sweet potatoes into large pieces. Put them in a glass or ceramic baking dish and top with thick slices of butter. Cover with foil and bake for 15 minutes.

Mix the brown sugar, cinnamon, nutmeg, and flour in a small bowl.

Remove the sweet potatoes from the oven and turn them over with a spatula. Sprinkle one third of the brown sugar mixture over them. Cover with foil and return to the oven for another 15 minutes.

Again remove the sweet potatoes from the oven and turn them. Sprinkle them with half the remaining brown sugar mixture. Cover and cook for another 15 minutes.

Once again, remove the sweet potatoes from the oven and turn them. Sprinkle the remaining brown sugar mixture over them. Cover and bake for another 15 minutes.

Remove the potatoes from the oven and turn them a final time. Sprinkle the potatoes with the pecans and currants. Leave the sweet potatoes uncovered and return them to the oven. Bake for a final ½ hour.

Yield: 6 to 8 servings

Pecan-Topped Twice-Baked Sweet Potatoes

4 medium sweet potatoes

Vegetable oil

½ cup pecans halves

¼ pound (1 stick) butter, at room temperature

½ cup light brown sugar

¼ cup breadcrumbs

Preheat the oven to 350 degrees.

Brush the sweet potatoes with oil. Put them on the middle rack in the oven and cook for 30 minutes until soft inside. Remove them from the oven and let cool.

Spread the pecans in a single layer on a baking sheet. Toast the pecans in the oven until they become oily and browned, 8 to 10 minutes. Remove the pecans from the oven and let cool.

Halve the potatoes lengthwise. Scoop out the potatoes into the bowl of a food processor, setting aside the skins. Add the butter, pecans, brown sugar, and breadcrumbs and process until smooth.

Reheat the oven to 375 degrees.

Put the potato skins on the middle rack and bake them until crisp, 10 to 12 minutes. Remove the skins and fill them with the potato mixture. Bake until brown and crisp. Serve immediately.

Yield: 4 servings

Braised Red Cabbage

1 tablespoon olive oil

4 thick slices country bacon, cut into 1 inch pieces

1 medium onion, sliced

½ cup balsamic vinegar

1½ teaspoons celery seed

1 small head purple cabbage, coarsely chopped

Fry the bacon in olive oil in a skillet over medium heat until it just begins to brown. Add the onion and sauté until it begins to soften. Add the vinegar and celery seed and stir until the liquid begins to boil.

Add the cabbage and continue to cook, stirring, until it is al dente—soft on the outside but still slightly crisp inside. Serve hot with pork or beef.

Yield: 6 to 8 servings

Red, White, and Black Baked Beans

6 slices peppered bacon, cooked and crumbled

1 tablespoon butter

1 large onion, chopped

½ cup apple cider vinegar

¾ cup barbecue sauce

⅓ cup dark molasses

⅓ cup water

1 tablespoon dry mustard

2 teaspoons dried thyme leaf

1 teaspoon kosher salt

1 teaspoon freshly ground pepper

1 (15-ounce) can red kidney beans, drained

1 (15-ounce) can black beans, drained

1 (15-ounce) can white kidney (cannellini) beans, drained

1 bay leaf

1 teaspoon Tabasco

Preheat the oven to 350 degrees.

Fry the bacon in an ovenproof pot over medium heat until crisp and golden brown. Drain it on paper towels.

Add the butter and chopped onion to the bacon drippings and sauté until the onion is tender. Stir in the cider vinegar, barbecue sauce, molasses, water, mustard, thyme, salt, pepper, bacon bits, and beans.

Add the bay leaf and cover the pot. Transfer the pot to the oven and bake for 1 hour. Stir every 15 minutes, adding a little water if necessary.

Stir in the Tabasco and remove the bay leaf.

Yield: 6 to 8 servings

Asparagus in Butter

You can easily double or triple this recipe; just be sure there are no more than two layers of asparagus, or it will not cook evenly. Use a second baking dish if necessary.

1 pound pencil thin asparagus spears
4 tablespoons (½ stick) butter, melted
Kosher salt and freshly ground pepper

Preheat the oven to 450 degrees.

Rinse and drain the asparagus. Snap off the tough ends where they break naturally.

Arrange the asparagus in a glass or ceramic baking dish in one or two layers.

Drizzle the butter over the asparagus and season with salt and pepper.

Cover the dish tightly with aluminum foil. Bake until tender, about 15 minutes, or longer to desired doneness. Serve at once.

Yield: 4 servings

Creamed Corn

5 tablespoons butter
⅓ cup all-purpose flour
1 cup heavy whipping cream
1 cup milk
¼ cup sugar
¼ teaspoon freshly grated nutmeg
1 teaspoon kosher salt
Pinch of ground white pepper
5 cups fresh or frozen corn, thawed
1 cup panko breadcrumbs
¼ cup grated Parmigiano-Reggiano cheese

Melt the butter in a large skillet over medium heat. Stir in the flour until smooth.

Gradually stir in the heavy cream and milk. Add the sugar, nutmeg, salt, and pepper.

Bring the mixture to a boil and continue stirring for 5 minutes.

Add the corn and stir until heated.

Transfer the mixture to an ungreased baking dish. Top with the panko breadcrumbs and Parmigiano-Reggiano cheese.

Broil until lightly browned and bubbly, 3 to 5 minutes.

Yield: 8 to 10 servings

Roasted Root Vegetables

Try this recipe on the grill, roasting the vegetables in a foil pouch instead of in a baking pan. The smoke from the grill imparts an excellent flavor to the vegetables.

8 cloves garlic, peeled and chopped

2 cups parsnips, sliced

2 cups baby carrots, rinsed

1 cup thinly sliced fennel bulb

2 medium red onions, peeled and cut into wedges

6 small red potatoes, rinsed and cut into wedges

1 cup sliced turnips

1 tablespoon fresh thyme leaves

Kosher salt and freshly ground pepper

¼ cup dry sherry

¼ cup olive oil

¼ cup chopped fresh parsley

Preheat the oven to 325 degrees.

Toss the vegetables in a mixing bowl.

Line the bottom of a baking sheet with parchment paper. Put the vegetables on the baking sheet and dust them with the thyme, salt, and pepper. Drizzle the sherry and olive oil over the vegetables.

Bake the vegetables in the middle of the oven for 1 hour, turning them after 30 minutes.

Remove the vegetables from the oven and sprinkle fresh parsley over them.

Yield: 6 to 8 servings

Mixed Grilled Vegetables

These are just suggestions; use as many vegetables or as few as you like, adding oil and salt before cooking. If it's too cold to grill, bake the vegetables in a 350-degree oven on a baking sheet lined with parchment paper.

1 zucchini, sliced into ½-inch thick rounds

1 summer squash, sliced ½-inch thick rounds

1 large onion, cut into chunks

1 red pepper, cut into strips

½ pound asparagus, stalks trimmed

1 small Japanese eggplant, sliced

¾ cup extra-virgin olive oil

1 teaspoon kosher salt

Prepare a grill for high heat.

Toss together the vegetables and olive oil in a large bowl.

Put the vegetables on a grilling rack or sheet of aluminum foil. Sprinkle salt over them. Place the rack on the grill directly over the heat.

Cook the vegetables for 3 to 5 minutes per side, turning them with tongs.

Yield: 6 to 8 servings

Cauliflower and Chestnuts Au Gratin

1 head cauliflower, florets and stems separated

3 tablespoons butter

⅓ cup shallots, finely chopped

3 cloves garlic, minced

Kosher salt

Freshly ground pepper

½ cup dry white wine

1 cup chicken stock

1 cup heavy cream

4 teaspoons prepared horseradish

Grated nutmeg

1 tablespoon fresh thyme leaves

3 cups grated Gruyère cheese

2 jars chestnuts, drained and quartered

Fresh chopped parsley

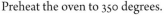

Preheat the oven to 350 degrees.

Bring a large pot of water to a boil. Cook the cauliflower florets in the water until tender, about 6 minutes. Drain the cauliflower and rinse it in cold water.

Chop the cauliflower stems to make 1½ cups.

Melt the butter in a large skillet over medium heat. Sauté the cauliflower stems, shallots, and garlic until the garlic begins to brown. Add salt and pepper to taste.

Add the white wine and chicken stock and bring it to a boil. Lower the heat and simmer until the liquid is reduced by half. Pour the mixure in a blender or food processor and purée until smooth.

Return the purée to the skillet over medium heat. Stir in the cream, horse-radish, nutmeg, and thyme. Add half the cheese and stir until melted.

Spread the cauliflower florets and chestnuts evenly in a 9 by 12-inch baking dish. Pour the sauce over them. Sprinkle the remaining cheese on top. Bake uncovered until the cheese is golden brown, 20 to 25 minutes. Garnish with parsley.

Yield: 6 to 8 servings

Ohio Summer Squash Casserole

3 tablespoons butter

⅓ cup chopped scallions

¾ cup diced celery

1 clove garlic, chopped

1 yellow summer squash, sliced ¼-inch thick (about 2 cups)

½ zucchini, sliced ¼-inch thick (about 1 cup)

1½ cups halved grape tomatoes

1 teaspoon kosher salt

½ teaspoon freshly ground pepper

1 tablespoon chopped fresh basil

Preheat the oven to 300 degrees.

Melt the butter in a saucepan over medium heat. Sauté the scallions, celery, and garlic until the scallions are soft and transparent. Stir in the summer squash and zucchini until blended, then remove the pan from the heat.

Transfer the mixture to a shallow casserole. Cover it with the grape tomatoes. Sprinkle the salt, pepper, and basil evenly on top.

Cover the casserole and bake for 40 minutes.

Yield: 6 to 8 servings

Creamy Squash Casserole

2 pounds summer squash, sliced
1 medium onion, chopped
1 carrot, sliced
1 cup sour cream
1 (10¾-ounce) can condensed cream of chicken soup
¼ pound (1 stick) butter, melted
Fresh croutons

Preheat the oven to 350 degrees.

Steam or boil the sliced squash until cooked, but still slightly crisp. Drain the squash and put it in a casserole.

Combine the onion, carrot, sour cream, chicken soup, and butter. Pour the mixture over the squash. Sprinkle croutons on top.

Bake until the top is golden brown, about 25 minutes.

Yield: 6 to 8 servings

Tomato and Corn Casserole

Ohio leads the country in the production of tomato juice and is second only to California in tomato growing. In 1965 the Ohio General Assembly even declared tomato juice the official state beverage. This recipe uses vine-ripened tomatoes and sweet corn, so it is a perfect accompaniment to a summer barbecue.

10 ears sweet corn
½ cup all-purpose flour
4 tablespoons (½ stick) butter
¾ cup breadcrumbs
⅓ cup extra-virgin olive oil
1 clove garlic, peeled and halved
6 large ripe tomatoes
1 large sweet onion, thinly sliced
Kosher salt and freshly ground pepper

Preheat the oven to 350 degrees.

Remove the husks and silk from the corn and rinse it. Cut the kernels off the cobs and put them in a bowl.

Crosscut the tomatoes into ½-inch slices.

Measure the flour into a pie pan or shallow bowl.

Melt the butter over medium heat in a large skillet. Sauté the breadcrumbs until golden brown. Remove the breadcrumbs from the skillet.

Return the skillet to medium heat, pour in the olive oil, and sauté the garlic until soft and golden. Remove the garlic from the skillet.

Dredge the tomato slices in the flour on both sides and fry them until just golden. Remove the skillet from the heat.

Lightly grease a large casserole with shortening. Place alternate layers of tomato, corn, and onion slices in it. Lightly season each layer with salt and pepper. Sprinkle the breadcrumbs evenly over the top layer.

Bake for 35 to 40 minutes.

Yield: 6 to 8 servings

Fresh Applesauce

As with most foods, fresh just tastes better. Applesauce is a natural with pork chops, pork roasts, and ham. At breakfast you can add it to hot oatmeal, spoon it over muesli, or serve it with hash-browned potatoes. Select a mixture of sweet and tart varieties of apple, for example Yellow Delicious, Granny Smith, and Braeburn.

12 to 15 mixed apples

2 cups apple cider or juice

Ground cinnamon and sugar to taste

Peel and core the apples. Cut them into eighths.

Bring the cider to a boil in a large saucepan over medium-high heat.

Put the apples in the saucepan and lower the heat to medium. Simmer until the apples reach the consistency of sauce, stirring frequently from the bottom of the pan. Keep the cooked apples on top of the mixture.

Stir in cinnamon and sugar to taste. Serve warm.

Yield: 12 to 14 servings

Sauerkraut-Stuffed Apples

3 tablespoons olive oil

1 clove garlic, minced

½ onion, thinly sliced

1 pound fresh sauerkraut, drained

2 tablespoons light brown sugar

3 tablespoons Hungarian sweet paprika

¾ cup water

½ bottle pale ale

6 large tart apples, rinsed

2 tablespoons dark brown sugar

1 tablespoon chopped pecans

Preheat the oven to 350 degrees.

Sauté the garlic in the olive oil in a large skillet over medium heat until it softens and begins to brown. Stir in the onion and sauerkraut. Stir in the brown sugar and paprika.

Lower the heat to simmer and add the water and beer. Cook until most of the liquid is gone.

Core the apples with a large diameter hole. Put the apples in a baking dish and stuff them with the sauerkraut mixture. Sprinkle brown sugar and chopped pecans over the apples. Bake for 10 minutes.

Serve warm over a small bed of the remaining sauerkraut.

Yield: 6 servings

Roasted Pineapple

1 large ripe pineapple, peeled and cored
4 tablespoons (½ stick) unsalted butter, melted
¾ cup packed light brown sugar
1 tablespoon vanilla powder

Preheat the oven to 400 degrees.

Slice the pineapple lengthwise into quarters. Crosscut each piece into 4 equal pieces to make 16 pineapple "steaks."

Put the pineapple on a baking sheet covered with parchment paper. Brush the butter on all sides of the pineapple. Sprinkle it with half the brown sugar and half the vanilla.

Bake the pineapple for 10 minutes. Remove it from the oven and turn the pieces. Sprinkle them with the remaining brown sugar and vanilla. Bake 5 minutes more.

Yield: 8 servings

Seafood

IN THE EARLY 1980s, most of the seafood available in Ohio was frozen. The idea that fresh fish at the store slept in the Chesapeake Bay the night before was a myth. Nowadays fishermen freeze it directly on the boat.

The McGinnis Sisters in Pittsburgh introduced me to the idea of directly air-freighting seafood from Boston into the Cleveland Airport. With their help, I met with Boston representatives and fishermen. Flying in our daily seafood needs gave us a two- to three-day freshness advantage over other retailers in the area. Fresh is what great quality seafood is all about.

Creamy Baked Halibut

We prefer flaky halibut but you will get excellent results with any whitefish, including cod, pollack, flounder, and sea bass.

½ cup chopped scallions with tops

1 cup sour cream

¼ teaspoon ground white pepper

½ teaspoon kosher salt

¼ teaspoon dill

2 pounds halibut fillets or thick steaks

⅓ cup grated Parmigiano-Reggiano cheese

Preheat the oven to 350 degrees.

Combine the scallions, sour cream, pepper, salt, and dill in a mixing bowl.

Put the halibut in a lightly greased baking pan. Spread the sour cream mixture evenly over the halibut. Bake the halibut for 25 minutes and remove it from the oven.

Turn on the broiler. Sprinkle the cheese over the fish. Broil until the cheese turns light golden brown, about 5 minutes.

Yield: 6 servings

Suggested wine: San Angelo Pinot Grigio, Banfi, Tuscany, Italy

Panko-Crusted Halibut with Spicy Aioli

Fifty years ago, when halibut was plentiful, it was the species of choice for fish and chips. In this recipe you pan-fry the fillets with an extra crispy coating of Japanese breadcrumbs and top them with a spicy aioli. Served with fried sweet fingerling potato wedges and a Tidewater cabbage slaw, it's fish and chips for a contemporary crowd.

AIOLI:

3 tablespoons mayonnaise

2 teaspoons fresh lime juice

2 tablespoons fresh cilantro

1 Serrano chili, seeded

1 garlic clove

HALIBUT:

1 cup milk

1 large egg

2 cups panko breadcrumbs

¼ cup all-purpose flour

½ teaspoon kosher salt

¼ teaspoon ground white pepper

4 (6-ounce) halibut fillets

Extra-virgin olive oil

1 tablespoon lime zest

Lemon wedges

Purée the mayonnaise, lime juice, cilantro, chili, and garlic in a blender until smooth and creamy. Cover and refrigerate.

Whisk the milk and egg in a mixing bowl until slightly foamy.

In another bowl, mix the breadcrumbs, flour, salt, and pepper.

Dredge both sides of the halibut in the milk and in the breadcrumb mix.

Coat the bottom of a large skillet with oil. Fry the breaded halibut over medium-high heat until the fish flakes easily with a fork, about 4 minutes per side.

Top with aioli and a sprinkling of lime zest. Serve with lemon wedges on the side.

Yield: 4 servings

Suggested wine: Soave Classico, Pieropan, Veneto, Italy

Nori Wrapped Cod

Nori is a paper-thin sheet of dried seaweed that is typically used to wrap sushi. In this recipe, we use it as a wrap for a cod and shrimp bundle that is sautéed and then finished in the oven. If you have trouble finding nori or you just want to experiment, use rice paper or won ton skins. Although the texture and flavor will be different, both are suitable for frying. Serve a good soy sauce on the side for dipping.

1 (2-pound) fresh cod fillet
Kosher salt and freshly ground pepper
1 lemon, sliced
1 sheet nori
4 medium shrimp, peeled and deveined
½ cup seasoned fine breadcrumbs
Olive oil
Fresh chopped parsley

Preheat the oven to 350 degrees.

Slice the cod into 4 even pieces. Season both sides with salt and pepper and squeeze a little lemon juice over the fillets.

Cut the nori lengthwise into 4 even strips. Place a cod fillet on the end of a strip of nori. Put a piece of shrimp on top of each cod fillet. Roll the nori around the cod and shrimp into a tight bundle, securing each bundle with a little water. Coat the exposed top and bottom of the fish with breadcrumbs. Repeat, wrapping the remaining cod and shrimp into nori bundles.

Coat the bottom of a medium skillet with olive oil and place it over medium heat. Sauté the cod wraps in the skillet, breadcrumb side down, until the breadcrumbs are golden brown, tuning once.

Remove the fish from the skillet and place it on a lightly greased baking pan. Finish cooking in the oven, 10 to 12 minutes.

Garnish with parsley and a slice of lemon.

Yield: 6 servings

Suggested wine: Pinot Blanc, Hugel, Alsace, France

Crispy Asiago Sea Bass

Panko is a kind of bread that originated in Japan around 1970. A unique dough mixture, special proofing, and induction baking—where the dough itself generates the heat via an electric current—all create an unusual loaf of bread with no crust and elongated crumbs. Panko crumbs have a coarse texture and unmatched crispness and flavor. Panko breadcrumbs can be found online and at better food stores.

½ cup coarse panko breadcrumbs

4 tablespoons finely grated Asiago cheese

3 tablespoons chopped fresh parsley

Zest of 1 lemon

3 garlic cloves, finely chopped

½ teaspoon kosher salt

½ teaspoon freshly ground pepper

2 teaspoons fresh lemon juice

Extra-virgin olive oil

4 sea bass fillets, about 6 ounces each

Preheat the oven to 400 degrees.

Combine the breadcrumbs, 3 tablespoons of the grated cheese, three quarters of the parsley, the lemon zest, garlic, salt, and pepper in a mixing bowl. Stir in the lemon juice and 2 to 3 tablespoons olive oil until the bread crumb mixture is moist.

Arrange the fillets in a lightly oiled baking pan. Spoon the bread crumb mixture evenly over the fillets, pressing down lightly. Lightly drizzle olive oil over the fillets.

Bake in the upper third of the oven until golden brown, about 15 minutes.

Top with a sprinkling of the remaining lemon zest and the remaining tablespoon of cheese.

Yield: 4 servings

Suggested wine: Ladybug White, Lolonis, Mendocino, California

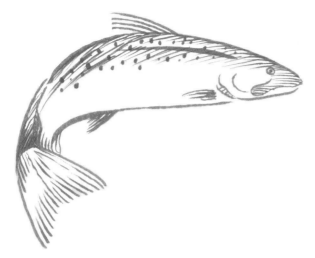

Grilled Wild Salmon with Honey-Wine Sauce

The season for fresh Alaskan salmon varies a little from year to year, depending on the number of fish that swim upriver to spawn. King salmon usually comes into season in the late spring, with Sockeye coming a month later, and Coho toward the end of the summer. If you can't get fresh wild salmon, you can use Washington State farmed salmon, though it won't have quite the flavor and texture of its wild cousins.

¼ cup wildflower honey

¼ cup chardonnay wine

1 tablespoon peeled and grated fresh ginger

2 tablespoons whole grain Dijon mustard

½ teaspoon kosher salt

½ teaspoon freshly ground black pepper

4 (6 to 8-ounce) wild salmon steaks

Combine the honey, wine, ginger, mustard, salt, and pepper in a small bowl until well mixed.

Dredge the salmon fillets in the mixture.

Place the salmon on the grill directly over high heat. Sear for 2 minutes, then turn the salmon. Baste the fillets with the sauce and continue to grill until the salmon flakes when pierced with a fork, 6 to 8 minutes.

Yield: 4 servings

Suggested wine: Riesling, Hans von Wilhelm Piesporter Goldtröpchen Spätlese, Mosel-Saar-Ruwer, Germany

Sweet Baked Salmon

This is the most foolproof method for cooking salmon. You wrap the fish in foil and cook it, skin side down, either in the oven or on the grill. The foil seals in the moisture and prevents any mess. When the salmon is done, you can easily separate the tender salmon flesh from the skin.

4 tablespoons (½ stick) butter

2 pounds salmon fillets

¼ cup brown sugar

Preheat the oven to 375 degrees.

Put two 1-tablespoon pats of butter on a large piece of aluminum foil. Place the salmon fillets over the butter, skin side down. Sprinkle the brown sugar evenly over the salmon. Place the remaining 2 pats of butter on top of the brown sugar. Cover the salmon with another sheet of foil. Fold and crimp the edges tightly together.

Put the salmon on a baking sheet and bake it in the oven until flaky when pierced with a fork, about 15 minutes.

Yield: 6 servings

Suggested wine: Riesling, Studert-Prüm Wehlener Sonnenuhr Kabinett, Mosel-Saar-Ruwer, Germany

Holiday Poached Salmon

We've made this elegant dish to order for years and, although it's a little involved, it's well worth the effort. Serve it with dill crème fraîche or Robert Rothschild's Chardonnay Mustard with added tarragon. For the ultimate in flavor, prepare this dish during the summer months, when fresh wild salmon is in season.

6 cups fish stock

½ bottle dry white wine

1 bag bouquet garni

1 (8 to 10-pound) whole salmon

1 large English cucumber, sliced paper-thin

¼ red onion, sliced paper thin

Fresh flowers and greens

To prepare the court-bouillon, bring the fish stock to a low boil in a large rectangular fish cooker. Add the wine and bouquet garni and allow to return to a boil.

Wrap the salmon in several layers of cheesecloth, leaving long ends of cloth to hang over the edges of the fish cooker. If you have a rack that fits in the fish cooker, use it to hold the salmon while poaching. If not, be careful not to split the salmon when lifting it from the liquid.

Lower the fish into the court-bouillon and lower the heat to just below the boiling point. Poach the salmon until a meat thermometer inserted into the thickest part of the salmon registers 160 degrees. Carefully remove the salmon and discard the liquid.

Put the salmon on a platter and cover it tightly with foil. Refrigerate until completely chilled.

Remove the salmon from the refrigerator. Using a thin knife, peel the top skin from the salmon, beginning below the head and proceeding toward the tail.

Overlap the cucumber slices on the exposed salmon meat to resemble scales. You will need enough cucumber to completely cover the salmon from just below the head to the fan of the tail. Place the separated onion rings around the neck and decorate the platter with fresh flowers and greens.

Serve with crème fraîche to which you've added chopped fresh dill (page 39). For a variation, coat the salmon with lemon Aioli (recipe follows) prior to placing the cucumber slices.

Yield: 32 to 40 servings

Lemon Aioli

1 cup mayonnaise
1 tablespoon lemon juice
1 teaspoon lemon zest
½ teaspoon kosher salt
¼ teaspoon sugar
1 clove garlic, finely chopped

Whisk the ingredients in a mixing bowl to form a smooth sauce. Cover tightly and keep refrigerated until ready to serve.

Yield: 1 cup

Three Pepper Walleye

1½ cups milk

1 teaspoon Tabasco

4 (6 to 8-ounce) walleye fillets

¾ cup yellow cornmeal

¼ cup all-purpose flour

1 teaspoon salt

¼ teaspoon garlic powder

1 teaspoon cracked black peppercorns

1 teaspoon ground white pepper

2 teaspoons cayenne pepper

Vegetable oil for frying

Fresh chopped parsley

Tartar sauce

To make the marinade, whisk the milk and Tabasco in a shallow baking dish. Put the walleye in the marinade. Cover and refrigerate for 4 to 8 hours, turning once.

Remove the fish from the refrigerator and let it stand at room temperature for 30 minutes.

Combine the cornmeal, flour, salt, garlic powder, and the three peppers in a bowl until well mixed. Pour ½ inch of vegetable oil in a heavy skillet, preferably cast iron, over medium-high heat.

Remove the fillets from the marinade and dredge them in to the cornmeal mix, coating both sides well. Fry the fillets to a golden brown.

Drain the fillets on paper towels. If needed, keep them in a warm oven while frying the rest of the batch.

Sprinkle the fillets lightly with chopped parsley and serve warm with tartar sauce.

Yield: 4 servings

Suggested wine: Macon-Villages, Joseph Drouhin, Burgundy, France

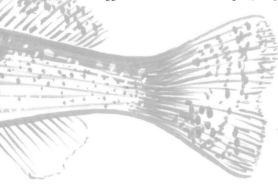

Buttermilk-Pecan Catfish

Clarified butter is butter from which the milk solids have been removed. It can be heated, without burning, to a much higher temperature than ordinary butter.

⅔ cup buttermilk

1 tablespoon Dijon mustard

Pinch of paprika

½ cup finely chopped pecans

½ cup all-purpose flour

¼ teaspoon kosher salt

¼ teaspoon ground nutmeg

1 pound of catfish fillets, cut into 1-inch pieces

¼ cup clarified butter (recipe follows)

Combine the buttermilk, mustard, and paprika in a small mixing bowl.

Combine the pecans, flour, salt, and nutmeg in a shallow bowl.

Heat the clarified butter in a heavy skillet over medium heat.

One at a time, drench the catfish fillets first in the buttermilk, then the flour, coating all sides.

Fry the catfish until golden brown, about 7 minutes, turning with tongs. Drain the fish on paper towels.

Yield: 2 to 4 servings

Suggested wine: Chardonnay, J. Lohr, Arroyo Seco, California

Clarified Butter

¼ pound (1 stick) of butter makes about ⅓ cup of clarified butter.

Slowly melt the butter in a small pan or measuring cup. Let it stand and separate for about fifteen minutes. Skim the foam off the top, then slowly pour off the clarified butter, leaving the visible milk solids on the bottom.

Friday Night at the Lake

Almond Coconut Scallops

As a variation, put the scallops on skewers and grill them. Serve with wild rice, asparagus, and plenty of butter.

12 fresh sea scallops

¼ cup thinly sliced almonds

¼ cup sweetened shredded coconut

Sea salt

12 slices of peppered bacon

Preheat the oven to 350 degrees.

Butterfly the scallops by slicing halfway through them and spreading them open like books.

Place equal portions of almonds and coconut on each scallop. Sprinkle them lightly with sea salt. Close the scallops back together to sandwich the almond and coconut topping inside.

Wrap the scallops with peppered bacon, securing the bacon with a toothpick.

Line a baking sheet with parchment paper and arrange the scallops on it.

Bake the scallops until they begin to turn golden, about 8 minutes.

Yield: 2 to 4 servings

Suggested wine: Viognier, Miner Family Vineyards, Oakville, California

Jamaican Shrimp and Plantains

Plantains are one variety of the cooking bananas popular in the Latin American tropics and Caribbean islands. Choose a large, green-skinned, firm plantain for this fairly spicy dish. If you prefer, chicken legs with the thighs attached may be substituted for the shrimp. Serve over wild rice.

2 tablespoons clarified butter (page 146)

1 teaspoon curry powder

1 ripe plantain, peeled and sliced into ½-inch pieces

1 pound of jumbo shrimp (15 count), peeled and deveined

Kosher salt

1 (4-ounce) jar Busha Browne's Authentic Jerk Seasoning

½ cup pineapple juice

½ medium onion, minced

¼ cup grated fresh coconut meat or dried flakes

1 cup wild rice, cooked

Mix the clarified butter and curry powder in a pan over medium heat. Add the plantains and sauté until golden brown. Drain the plantains on paper towels.

Put the shrimp in the pan. Sprinkle lightly with salt and jerk seasoning. Sauté the shrimp until they turn light orange.

Stir in the pineapple juice and the onion. Cover and lower the heat. Simmer for 10 minutes.

Add the coconut and plantains to the shrimp. Stir, cooking, until the mixture thickens.

Serve over cooked wild rice.

Yield: 2 to 4 servings

Suggested wine: Côtes-du-Rhône Rosé, Domaine de la Mordorée, Southern Rhone, France

Baked Crab and Shrimp

This seafood and vegetable medley can be baked either in a single casserole or in four to six individual soufflé dishes. It's perfect in the summertime with corn on the cob and herbed butter.

2 tablespoons butter

1 medium onion, chopped

1 green bell pepper, seeded and chopped

1 cup finely chopped celery

1 cup flaked crab meat

1 pound medium shrimp, peeled and deveined

1 cup mayonnaise

1 teaspoon Worcestershire sauce

½ teaspoon kosher salt

¼ teaspoon freshly ground pepper

¼ cup panko breadcrumbs

Preheat the oven to 350 degrees.

Melt the butter in a small skillet over medium heat. Sauté the onions, peppers, and celery until the onion is soft.

Stir together the crabmeat, shrimp, mayonnaise, Worcestershire sauce, salt, and pepper in a mixing bowl. Stir in the cooked vegetables.

Transfer the mixture to a lightly greased casserole and sprinkle with breadcrumbs.

Bake for 30 minutes.

Yield: 4 to 6 servings

Suggested wine: Unoaked Chardonnay, Kim Crawford, Marlborough, New Zealand

Poultry

ONE OF THE most popular dishes, available fresh or frozen, is our pot pie. I found the secret in the kitchen of a large food store in St. Louis. Their most popular item, pinched crust pies, was selling by the hundreds. Thinking about the enormous amount of hand labor involved, I questioned them about how they kept up with production. The chef shared his secret: a local pie company made a savory dough, formed in a five-inch pan with a raw dough disk for the top. All the store had to do was make the quality chicken breast filling and bake it.

We use the same idea now, with hundreds of pinch crusts made here in our own bakery and filled with top-quality, plump and juicy Ohio-grown chicken, direct from Amish country. To distinguish the chicken pot pie from the beef pot pie, we use little cookie-cutter cutouts of cows or chickens and bake them on the top. It's just another one of the little personal touches people remember us by.

Chicken Pot Pie

½ pound boneless, skinless chicken breast

¼ pound boneless, skinless chicken thigh

1 West Point Market Pie Crust (page 224)

1 egg

2 cups plus 2 tablespoons water

2 teaspoons chicken base

⅓ cup diced carrot

⅓ cup diced celery

2 tablespoons diced onion

¼ cup sliced button mushrooms

⅛ teaspoon celery seed

¼ teaspoon dried thyme leaves

2 tablespoons butter

2 tablespoons all-purpose flour

2 tablespoons frozen peas

Preheat the oven to 350 degrees.

Put the chicken in a baking pan lined with parchment paper. Bake for 10 minutes per side, turning once. Remove the chicken from the oven and let cool. Dice the chicken into ½-inch cubes.

Raise the oven temperature to 375 degrees.

Divide the pie crust dough in half. On a lightly floured surface, roll each half into an 11-inch circle. Place one circle of dough in a 9-inch pie pan. Cover the pie shell and the other circle of dough and set them aside.

To make egg wash, whisk the egg and the 2 tablespoons of the water in a small mixing bowl until smooth and frothy. Set it aside in the refrigerator.

Dissolve the chicken base in the remaining 2 cups of water in a stockpot over medium heat. Add the carrot, celery, onion, mushroom, celery seed, and thyme. Bring to a boil.

Make a basic roux in a small skillet. Melt the butter over medium heat. Add the flour to the center of the pan and stir with the butter until smooth, foamy, and slightly browned.

Remove the skillet from the heat and add the roux to the still simmering stockpot, stirring constantly until smooth. Continue to simmer, stirring, for about 10 minutes while the mixture thickens.

Remove the stockpot from the heat and stir in the peas. Pour the pie filling into the dough-lined pie pan. Place the other circle of dough over the pie. Crimp the edges to seal. Brush the top with egg wash.

Bake the pie until the top crust is golden brown in the center, about 40 minutes.

Yield: 2 to 4 servings

Roast Chicken

1 (4-pound) whole roasting chicken
Fresh Herb Brine for Poultry (recipe follows)
1 tablespoon dried rosemary
1 tablespoon dried thyme leaf
1 tablespoon olive oil
2 cups chicken stock

Rinse the chicken. Cover it with brine in a large stockpot. Cover the stockpot and refrigerate overnight.

Preheat the oven to 375 degrees.

Lift the chicken out of the brine and rinse it under cold water. Dry it with paper towels.

Put the chicken in a roasting pan. Stir the rosemary, thyme, and olive oil directly into the chicken stock and pour it into the pan. Roast the chicken on a lower rack for 15 minutes.

Lower the temperature to 325 degrees and cook the chicken an additional 1¼ hours. Baste the chicken with the pan juices every 20 minutes. Add more stock to the roasting pan, if needed. If the chicken browns too quickly, cover it loosely with foil. Remove the foil during the last 15 minutes to finish the browning.

Use a meat thermometer to test for doneness. Insert it deep into the thigh, not touching any bone. The chicken is done when the thigh temperature reads 160 to 165 degrees and the juices run clear, with no tinge of pink.

Allow the chicken to rest out of the oven for 10 to 15 minutes.

Yield: 4 to 6 servings

Fresh Herb Brine for Poultry

1 gallon water
1 cup sugar
1 cup kosher salt
1 bunch fresh sage, finely chopped
1 bunch fresh thyme, finely chopped
3 tablespoons cracked black pepper

Pour the water into a large pot. Stir in the seasonings and simmer over medium heat until the salt and sugar are dissolved. Chill.

Submerge the chicken or turkey in the brine. Cover with plastic wrap and refrigerate. If it is not totally submerged, turn the bird in the brine after 12 hours. Let the bird steep for 24 hours in all.

Yield: 1 gallon

Classic Creamed Chicken

Use our roast chicken recipe (page 154) or, if you're in a hurry, buy a whole cooked rotisserie chicken from a deli and cut it into wings, legs, thighs, and breasts.

6 tablespoons (¾ stick) butter

6 tablespoons all-purpose flour

1 teaspoon kosher salt

½ teaspoon ground white pepper

1 cup heavy cream

1½ cups chicken broth

2 tablespoons dry sherry

1 cut-up roasted chicken (page 154) or cooked rotisserie chicken, with skin

Melt the butter in a large skillet over medium heat. Whisk in the flour, salt, and pepper until it foams.

Add the heavy cream in a continuous stream while whisking. Add the broth in the same manner. Bring the sauce to a boil, then lower the heat.

Add the sherry and continue to simmer. Put the chicken in the skillet and stir gently to coat it with the cream sauce. Continue to simmer, stirring occasionally, until the sauce thickens.

Yield: 4 to 6 servings

Suggested wine: Pinot Gris, A to Z, Newberg, Oregon

Red Mole Rotisserie Chicken

This Mexican mole, a rich, dark, reddish-brown sauce, can be prepared in advance and frozen for up to a month, until the just the right chicken comes along.

4 whole dried ancho chilies

1 large dried chipotle pepper

2 small ripe tomatoes, halved, seeded, and cored

½ cup unsalted peanuts

1½ teaspoons allspice berries

½ teaspoon whole cloves

1 teaspoon black peppercorns

2 tablespoons peanut oil

1 ripe plantain, quartered

3 tablespoons extra-virgin olive oil

1 tablespoon ground cinnamon stick

2 ounces Mexican baking chocolate or bittersweet chocolate

1½ teaspoons sherry vinegar

1 cup chicken stock

Kosher salt

1 cut-up roasted chicken (page 154) or cooked rotisserie chicken, with skin

Preheat the oven to 400 degrees.

Place the ancho and chipotle chilies in a small bowl of hot water. Let them soften for 20 minutes.

Line a baking sheet with parchment paper. Put the tomato pieces on the baking sheet, flesh-side down. Roast for 10 minutes. Add the peanuts, allspice, cloves, and peppercorns and roast for another 10 minutes. Remove the tomatoes from the oven. Let them cool, then remove and discard their skins.

Slice open the softened chilies and remove the seeds and stems.

Heat the peanut oil in a medium skillet over high heat. Sauté the plantain pieces until browned. Drain them on paper towels.

Using the flat side of a chef's knife, crush the roasted allspice, cloves, peppercorns, and cinnamon stick into small, cracked pieces on a cutting board.

Purée the chilies in a blender or food processor. Add the crushed spices, peanuts, and plantains. Blend the mixture to a paste.

Heat the olive oil in a skillet over medium-high heat. Stir in the chilies and plantain paste. Lower the heat and simmer for 10 minutes, stirring. Add the chocolate and stir until melted. Add the vinegar and chicken stock. Simmer, stirring, for 5 minutes. Season with salt to taste.

Serve the chicken on a bed of white rice with a generous ladle of mole sauce.

Yield: 4 to 6 servings

Suggested wine: Garnacha Viña Borgia, Bodegas Borsao, Campo de Borja, Spain

Lemon Chicken Scaloppine

Scaloppine is the Italian term for small, thin, pieces of meat. Although we use chicken breast, you can substitute thinly sliced veal cutlets.

4 whole boneless, skinless chicken breasts

¼ cup all-purpose flour

2 tablespoons extra-virgin olive oil

⅓ cup dry white wine

¼ teaspoon dried thyme

¼ cup heavy cream

1 teaspoon lemon juice

Kosher salt and freshly ground pepper

1 tablespoon chopped fresh parsley

Place the chicken between wax paper or plastic wrap and gently pound it with the flat side of a mallet or cleaver to a ¼-inch thickness. Dust both sides of the chicken with flour.

Heat the oil in a large skillet over medium heat. Fry the chicken until browned on both sides, 3 to 5 minutes. Cover and keep warm in a 300-degree oven.

Pour the white wine in the skillet and let it boil, scraping (deglazing) the bottom and sides of the pan. Add the thyme.

When the wine has reduced by half, add the heavy cream and lemon juice. Continue to stir until the sauce is thickened, about 5 minutes. Add salt and pepper to taste.

To serve, spoon the sauce over the chicken and add a pinch of parsley.

Yield: 4 servings

Suggested wine: Kris Pinot Grigio, Franz Haas, Venezie, Italy

Chicken with Plantains and Pineapple Sauce

¼ cup brown sugar

1 cup pineapple juice

1 cup fresh orange juice

3 tablespoons soy sauce

2 cloves garlic, minced

½ teaspoon ginger

¼ cup sherry

Zest of ½ orange

8 chicken legs with thighs attached

2 cups crushed pineapple

1 tablespoon Madagascar Bourbon vanilla extract

4 tablespoons (½ stick) butter, melted

¾ cup sugar

1 stick cinnamon

2 ripe plantains

¼ cup vegetable oil

½ teaspoon salt

Mix the brown sugar, ½ cup of the pineapple juice, the orange juice, soy sauce, garlic, ginger, sherry, and orange zest in a bowl. Add the chicken to the marinade, making sure it is covered. Cover tightly with plastic wrap and refrigerate for 4 hours.

Preheat the oven to 350 degrees.

For the pineapple sauce, combine the crushed pineapple, vanilla, butter, sugar, cinnamon, and the remaining ½ cup of pineapple juice in a saucepan over low heat. Stir and simmer for 20 minutes.

Put the marinated chicken in a large baking pan. Bake uncovered for 30 minutes, basting with the marinade.

Quarter the plantains lengthwise. Slice each quarter into half-lengths, making 8 equal pieces.

Heat the oil in a large skillet over medium-high heat. Carefully lay the plantain slices in the oil and fry them until crisp, turning often so they brown evenly. Drain the plantains on paper towels. Salt them lightly.

To serve, remove the cinnamons stick and spoon the pineapple sauce on the plantains and chicken.

Yield: 8 servings

Suggested wine: Evolution Lucky Number 9, Sokol Blosser Winery, Dundee, Oregon

Grilled Chicken with Cherry Chipotle Sauce

1 tablespoon olive oil

2 cloves garlic, minced

½ cup chopped shallots

2 tablespoons balsamic vinegar

⅓ cup red wine

2 tablespoons canned chipotle chilies, minced

½ cup dried tart cherries, chopped

½ cup tart cherry preserves

1 teaspoon cumin

Kosher salt and freshly ground pepper

6 chicken breasts, bone-in, with skin

Sauté the garlic and shallots in a skillet over medium heat until the garlic just browns and begins to soften.

Stir in the vinegar, wine, chilies, cherries, preserves, and cumin. Bring the mixture to a boil and lower the heat. Cover and simmer for 20 minutes.

Sprinkle salt and pepper on the chicken and grill it over high heat until golden brown.

To serve, spoon the sauce over the chicken.

Yield: 6 to 8 servings

Suggested wine: Grenache/Shiraz, Hill of Content, South Australia

Chicken Satay with Peanut Sauce

Satay are kebabs composed of small cubes or strips of marinated meat, poultry, or seafood on bamboo skewers. Served with a spicy peanut sauce on the side, they're a fast-food snack common among vendors at open-air markets in southeast Asia. Grill satay over very hot coals or on high heat on a gas grill, turning them frequently and being careful not to burn the skewers.

PEANUT SAUCE:

½ cup chopped scallions

⅓ cup chopped fresh cilantro leaves plus additional for garnish

2 Serrano chilies, seeded and chopped

2 cloves garlic, minced

1 teaspoon minced ginger

12 ounces peanut butter, preferably freshly-made

2 tablespoons sesame oil

1 tablespoon fresh lime juice

2 tablespoons Hoisin sauce

1 can of unsweetened coconut milk

CHICKEN SATAY:

¼ cup soy sauce

3 tablespoons peanut oil

1 teaspoon honey

3 cloves garlic, chopped

2 teaspoons fresh ginger

1 tablespoon Madras curry powder

1 teaspoon ground coriander

½ teaspoon red pepper flakes

Zest of 1 lime

8 boneless, skinless chicken breasts, cut into strips

For the peanut sauce, combine the scallions, cilantro, chilies, garlic, and ginger in a food processor or blender and mix on high speed for 30 seconds.

Scrape down the sides of the container and add the peanut butter, sesame oil, lime juice, and Hoisin sauce. Blend for another 30 seconds. Again scrape down the sides.

With the blender running, slowly pour in the coconut milk and process the peanut sauce until smooth, scraping down the sides as needed.

Cover and refrigerate.

Stir together all the ingredients except the chicken in a large mixing bowl until well blended. Add the chicken and cover the bowl tightly with a lid or plastic wrap. Refrigerate for 4 hours.

Thread the marinated chicken strips onto skewers. Grill the chicken over high heat for 3 to 4 minutes per side, turning once.

Arrange the skewers on a platter and drizzle the chicken lightly with peanut sauce. Garnish with fresh cilantro. Serve the remaining sauce on the side.

Yield: 8 servings

Suggested wine: Richter Riesling Estate, Weingut Max Ferd. Richter, Mosel-Saar-Ruwer, Germany

Panko-Crusted Baked Chicken

3 cups buttermilk

3 tablespoons Tabasco or other hot pepper sauce

4 tablespoons kosher salt

6 boneless, skinless chicken breasts

1 cup all-purpose flour

1 tablespoon freshly ground black pepper

1 tablespoon dried chili pepper

1 tablespoon Hungarian paprika

1 tablespoon mustard powder

2 teaspoons dried thyme

3 large eggs

2 cups panko breadcrumbs

The day before cooking, prepare the marinade. Stir together the buttermilk, Tabasco, and 3 tablespoons of the kosher salt. Rinse the chicken breasts and pat them dry. Put the chicken in the marinade and cover the bowl with an airtight lid or plastic wrap. Refrigerate overnight.

Preheat the oven to 350 degrees.

Stir together the flour, the remaining tablespoon of salt, the black pepper, chili powder, paprika, mustard powder, and thyme in a mixing bowl until well blended.

Whisk the eggs in another mixing bowl until foamy.

Put the breadcrumbs in a third mixing bowl. Line a baking sheet with parchment paper.

One at a time, put the chicken breasts in the flour mixture, coating both sides well, then dredge them in the egg and put them in the breadcrumbs to coat them completely.

Put the breadcrumb-coated chicken breasts on the baking sheet and bake until golden brown, 35 to 45 minutes.

Yield: 6 servings

Suggested wine: Riesling, Robert Mondavi Private Selection, Monterey County, California

Mediterranean Grilled Chicken

2 tablespoons vegetable oil

½ cup chopped red onion

2 cloves garlic, chopped

1 teaspoon powdered ginger

1 Serrano chili or other small, hot pepper, stemmed, seeded, and finely chopped

1 tablespoon Hungarian paprika

1½ teaspoons kosher salt

1 teaspoon ground cumin

1 teaspoon turmeric

1 teaspoon ground coriander

1 teaspoon garam masala

½ teaspoon cayenne pepper

½ cup plain yogurt

1 tablespoon lemon juice

1 chicken, skin removed, cut into pieces

Nan or pita flatbread

Major Grey's chutney

Combine the oil, onion, garlic, ginger, Serrano chili, paprika, salt, cumin, turmeric, coriander, garam masala, and cayenne in a blender or food processor. Blend on high to make a paste.

Scrape down the sides and add the yogurt and lemon juice. Blend to turn the paste into a smooth sauce.

Use a fork to poke holes in the chicken to allow the marinade to soak in. Put the chicken in a mixing bowl or container. Pour the marinade over the chicken. Cover and refrigerate for 12 hours, turning the chicken once.

Grill the chicken bone-side down over high heat, but not directly over the flame or coals. Just before the chicken is done, heat the flatbread on the grill for 2 minutes directly over the flame or coals, turning once.

Serve the chicken with warm flatbread and sweet tamarind chutney as a condiment.

Yield: 4 to 6 servings

Suggested wine: Gewurztraminer, Husch, Anderson Valley, California

Creamed Artichoke and Feta Chicken

4 whole boneless, skinless chicken breasts

2 cloves of garlic, peeled and finely chopped

1 medium onion, diced

½ cup scallion, diced

⅓ cup olive oil

1 (12-ounce) can of artichoke hearts in water, drained

¼ cup dry white wine

1 pint heavy cream

½ cube chicken bouillon

1 pound of feta cheese, crumbled

Salt and freshly ground pepper

¼ cup chopped fresh parsley

Grill the chicken breasts over hot coals or high heat on a gas grill. Remove the chicken from the grill and chop it into medium pieces.

Sauté the garlic, onion, and scallions in a large skillet over medium-high heat for 2 minutes. Add the chicken, artichokes, and wine. Simmer for 5 minutes.

Warm the cream in a saucepan over medium heat, stirring. Add the chicken bouillon and continue to stir until the cream is reduced by a quarter. Add ¾ cup of the feta and stir until well blended. Pour the mixture into the skillet and return the pan to the heat. Add salt and pepper to taste. Stir the mixture another 3 to 5 minutes.

Serve with fresh parsley and the remaining feta cheese sprinkled on top.

Yield: 4 servings

Suggested wine: Domaine de Valmoissine Pinot Noir, Maison Louis Latour, Coteaux du Verdon, France

Lemon Artichoke Chicken

6 boneless, skinless chicken breasts cut lengthwise into ¾-inch strips

3 tablespoons extra-virgin olive oil

1 (16-ounce) can artichoke hearts, drained and quartered

½ cup chicken broth

3 tablespoons lemon juice

1½ cups roasted red pepper strips

6 ounce baby Portobello mushrooms

¼ cup Kalamata olives, halved

¼ cup dry white wine

Chopped fresh parsley

Heat the olive oil in a skillet over medium heat. Sauté the chicken strips for about 8 minutes. Remove the chicken from the skillet and set it aside.

Put the artichoke hearts, chicken broth, lemon juice, peppers, mushrooms, olives, and white wine in the skillet. Reduce the liquid over medium-high heat, stirring and scraping the pan often, about 10 minutes.

Serve the chicken over the vegetable mixture and garnish with fresh parsley.

Yield: 6 servings

Suggested wine: Riesling, Huia, Marlborough, New Zealand

Coconut Curry Chicken with Rice

ORANGE RICE:

    1 cup water

    1½ cups orange juice

    1 tablespoon grated orange peel

    1 teaspoon salt

    1 cup basmati long grain rice

COCONUT CURRY CHICKEN:

    ¼ cup olive oil

    2½ pounds boneless, skinless chicken breast, cubed

    Salt and freshly ground pepper

    1 large onion, chopped

    1 yellow bell pepper, sliced into thin strips

    1 tablespoon Madras Curry Powder

    1 cup of canned San Marzano plum tomatoes

    1 cup canned unsweetened coconut milk

    Fresh basil

Combine all the rice ingredients in a saucepan and bring to a boil over medium-high heat. Turn the heat off, cover the pan, and let stand 1 hour.

Heat the olive oil in a deep skillet over medium-high heat. Season the chicken with salt and pepper. Sear the chicken breasts on all sides, about 8 minutes. Remove the chicken from the skillet and set it aside.

Sauté the onions and peppers over medium heat until tender, about 6 minutes. Stir in the curry powder. Return the chicken to the skillet. Using your hands, crush the tomatoes in the skillet. Pour in the coconut milk and add salt and pepper to taste.

Bring the chicken mixture to a boil. Lower the heat and simmer for about 15 minutes, allowing the sauce to thicken and the flavors to develop. Garnish with basil and serve over orange rice.

Yield: 6 servings

Suggested wine: Vouvray, Barton & Guestier, Loire Valley, France

Herb-Roasted Turkey

1 (12-14 lb.) fresh whole turkey
¼ pound (1 stick) unsalted butter, softened
½ teaspoon garlic powder
½ teaspoon thyme leaf
½ teaspoon rosemary
¼ teaspoon sage
¼ cup extra-virgin olive oil
1 tablespoon lemon juice
4 cups turkey stock
1 recipe Fresh Herb Brine for Poultry (page 154)

At least 24 hours before cooking, brine the turkey.

Preheat the oven to 375 degrees.

Blend the butter, garlic, thyme, rosemary, sage, olive oil, and lemon juice. Transfer the mixture to a small pastry bag or ziplock plastic bag and refrigerate it.

Lift the turkey out of the brine and rinse it under cold water. Dry it with paper towels. Slide a small rubber spatula between the skin and the breast meat to separate them. Using your hand, continue to separate the skin from the meat, opening a large cavity.

Pipe half the herb butter under the skin of both breasts, using your fingertips to spread it evenly. Rub the remaining herb butter on the outside of the bird.

Put the turkey in a roasting pan. Add 1 cup of stock and roast on a low oven rack for 1½ hours.

Lower the heat to 325 degrees. For a 12-pound turkey, roast for an additional 1½ hours, 2 hours if the turkey is stuffed. Cook another 30 minutes for each additional 2 pounds.

If the turkey browns too quickly, cover it loosely with foil. Remove the foil during the last ½ hour to finish the browning. Add more stock to the roasting pan during cooking, if needed.

Use a meat thermometer to test for doneness. Insert it deep into the thigh, not touching any bone. The turkey is done when the temperature reads 160 degrees to 165 degrees and the juices run clear yellow, with no tinge of pink. For a stuffed turkey, insert the thermometer deep into the stuffing.

Allow the turkey to rest out of the oven for 20 minutes. Its temperature will rise another 5 to 10 degrees and it will be easier to carve.

Yield: 12 to 14 servings

Suggested wine: Meritage, Estancia, Paso Robles, California

Turkey Roasting Times

Approximate total cooking times
375 degree/325 degree oven as recommended on page 167

Weight	Unstuffed Birds	Stuffed Birds
9–12 pounds	2½ to 3 hours	3 to 3½ hours
12–14 pounds	3 to 3½ hours	3½ to 4 hours
14–18 pounds	3½ to 4 hours	4 to 4½ hours
18–20 pounds	4 to 4½ hours	4½ to 5 hours
20–23 pounds	4½ to 5 hours	5 to 5½ hours
23–26 pounds	5 to 5¼ hours	5½ to 6 hours
26+ pounds	5¼ to 5¾ hours	5¾ to 6¼ hours

Turkey Braciola

We challenged our executive chef, Tom Loraditch, to create something really different for customers who had become bored with traditional roast turkey. This special dish just might become your family's tradition!

1 (4-pound) double lobe boneless fresh turkey breast, with skin,
    or 1 (6-pound) bone-in fresh turkey breast, bone removed, with skin

1 cup muffaletta olive spread

¾ pound veal scallopine

¼ pound provolone cheese, thinly sliced

¾ pound cooked chopped spinach

½ pound roasted red pepper strips

½ pound porchetta (deli pork loin), thinly sliced

1 pound bulk Italian sausage

Fontina Supreme Sauce (recipe follows)

Preheat the oven to 350 degrees.

Place the boneless turkey breast skin side down on a cutting board and butterfly each lobe so the meat lies flat. Layer the remaining ingredients evenly on the turkey in the order listed above. Place the sausage toward the center in a long strip.

Carefully roll the turkey into a bundle, tucking the sides into the roll. Secure the braciola with butcher's twine. Put the roll in a roasting pan over a sheet of parchment paper.

Bake for 45 minutes. Lower the heat to 300 degrees and continue to cook until a meat thermometer inserted in the center reads 145 degrees, another 45-60 minutes. Remove the braciola from the oven and let it rest 10 minutes.

Remove the butcher's twine and slice the braciola into generous portions. Serve with Fontina Supreme sauce.

Yield: 14 to 18 servings

Fontina Supreme Sauce

4 tablespoons (½ stick) melted butter

3 tablespoons all-purpose flour

2 cups chicken stock

1 cup heavy cream

6 ounces shredded Italian fontina cheese

Kosher salt and ground white pepper

Melt the butter over medium heat. Whisk in the flour until it is light tan in color and has a nutty aroma, 5 to 7 minutes.

Add the chicken stock while continuing to whisk. Lower the heat and let the mixture simmer for 15 minutes. Add the cream and fontina cheese and stir until the cheese is melted and the mixture is smooth.

Add salt and ground white pepper to taste.

Yield: 4 cups

Thanksgiving Dinner

Meats

OUR BUSINESS started from the "center of the plate," the most important part of the meal. The "center of the plate" is the meat; a good chef builds the meal around it. In the early 1900s, John Seiler, a German butcher, arrived in Akron. He started out working at a small butcher shop in Firestone Park, but soon moved on to the finest store in the city, Fred Wecker's Highland Square Market. He had a leased meat department in the store, and offered the quality that the high-income business and professional customers in the area appreciated. John developed a serious reputation for top quality meats. After the stock market crash, times being what they were, John's rent was doubled. That Saturday night John invited two of his most promising clerks, Harold Vernon and Harry Anderson, to his house for dinner and a beer. After the bean soup, he asked them to join him in a risky venture. They agreed, putting down $500 each, and opened their new store only four blocks away, naming it after the intersection of Merriman Road and West Market Street. John's loyal customers followed the "center of the plate" down the street to his new Point Market, as it was known then, and have stayed with him for the past seventy years.

Stuffed Banana Peppers

1 tablespoon olive oil

3 cloves garlic, minced

1 pound Italian sausage, casing removed

2 cups panko breadcrumbs

2 eggs

1 cup chicken broth

½ cup grated pepper jack cheese

½ cup grated Parmigiano-Reggiano cheese

½ cup grated pecorino Romano cheese

½ cup grated mozzarella cheese

Kosher salt and freshly ground pepper

6 large banana peppers, seeded

Preheat the oven to 350 degrees.

Sauté the garlic in olive oil in a skillet over medium heat until it just begins to brown and soften. Add the sausage and stir to break up the meat and keep it from sticking. Brown the sausage. Strain the sausage and garlic mix to remove the grease.

Mix half the breadcrumbs and 1 egg. Stir in the cooked sausage and chicken broth. Add the four cheeses and stir until all the ingredients are well mixed. Add salt and pepper to taste.

Whisk the remaining 2 eggs until foamy in another bowl. Put the remaining breadcrumbs in a third bowl.

Dredge the banana peppers in the egg and coat them with breadcrumbs.

Fill the peppers with the sausage and cheese mix. Put the peppers in a baking dish lined with parchment paper and bake them for 35 to 40 minutes.

Yield: 5 servings

Raspberry Chipotle Chorizo Pie

This recipe uses West Point Market's raspberry chipotle sauce. To make your own, pour 1 cup of mild (no smoke) barbecue sauce into a blender. Add frozen or dried raspberries, a tablespoon at a time, and purée the mixture. Continue adding raspberries to taste. Add ½ teaspoon dried chipotle peppers per cup of sauce. Use your raspberry chipotle sauce as a finishing glaze on beef, pork, or chicken.

1 tablespoon extra-virgin olive oil
½ bunch chopped scallions with tops
1 shallot, diced
2 cloves garlic, chopped
1 (15-ounce) can pinto beans, rinsed and drained
¼ cup corn kernels
1 cup mild chunky salsa
½ cup raspberry chipotle sauce
½ teaspoon cumin
1 teaspoon chili powder
1¼ pounds cooked chorizo sausage, sliced ½ inch thick
½ teaspoon kosher salt
½ teaspoon freshly ground pepper
6 corn tortillas, quartered
3 cups grated white Mexican cheese (queso blanco)

Preheat the oven to 350 degrees.

Sauté the scallions, shallot, and garlic a large skillet over medium heat until the garlic just begins to brown. Add the beans, corn, salsa, chipotle sauce, cumin, chili powder, chorizo, salt, and pepper. Lower the heat and let the mixture simmer until it thickens, stirring occasionally.

Arrange half the tortilla pieces over the bottom and sides of a 9-inch pie plate. Spoon half the filling evenly over the tortillas. Sprinkle half the grated cheese over the filling. Place the remaining tortillas in another layer over the cheese, then add the remaining filling and the remaining cheese.

Bake the tortilla pie until the cheese is brown and the pie is heated throughout, about 20 minutes. Remove the pie from the oven and let it set for 10 to 15 minutes before serving.

Yield: 4 to 6 servings

Suggested wine: Tres Picos Garnacha, Bodegas Borsao, Campo De Borja, Spain

Panfried Italian Sausage and Grapes

    3 tablespoons extra-virgin olive oil

    2 pounds sweet Italian sausage links, cut into 4-inch pieces

    2½ pounds of assorted red, green, and black seedless grapes, stems removed

    ⅓ cup balsamic vinegar

    Kosher salt and freshly ground pepper

Heat the olive oil in a sauté pan over medium heat. Sauté the sausage, turning often, until browned on all sides.

Add the grapes and cook until softened, 10 to 15 minutes.

Drizzle balsamic vinegar over the sausage and grapes. Add the salt and pepper and continue to cook on low heat while the vinegar reduces slightly.

Yield: 4 to 6 servings

Suggested wine: Barbera, Seghesio Family Vineyards, Healdsburg, California

Old-Fashioned Meatballs in Tomato Sauce

Traditional tomato sauces for pasta are often based on simple recipes with few added seasonings. Flavors are infused into this sauce by simmering savory meatballs and sausages over low, slow heat. This delicious recipe will have your guests convinced that you're Italian.

1 pound lean ground sirloin

½ pound sweet Italian sausage, casing removed

⅓ cup unflavored dry breadcrumbs

2 eggs, lightly beaten

2 large cloves garlic, minced

¼ cup plus 2 tablespoons grated pecorino Romano cheese

½ teaspoon salt

1 teaspoon freshly ground pepper

1 tablespoon chopped fresh basil

1 tablespoon chopped fresh parsley

2 cups crushed San Marzano plum tomatoes in purée

⅓ cup plus ¼ cup water

Let the ground sirloin and Italian sausage sit at room temperature, covered, for 30 to 60 minutes.

Preheat the oven to 425 degrees.

Put the breadcrumbs in a large bowl. Stir in ⅓ cup of water. Gently mix in the eggs, garlic, ¼ cup of the cheese, the salt, pepper, basil, and parsley.

Add the ground sirloin and Italian sausage and mix until completely blended. Form and roll the mixture with your hands into 10 even-sized meatballs, about 2½-inches each.

Place the meatballs about 1 inch apart in a 9 by 13-inch baking dish.

Stir ¼ cup of water into the crushed tomatoes and season with salt and freshly ground pepper. Pour the tomato sauce over the meatballs. Sprinkle the remaining 2 tablespoons of cheese on the meatballs.

Bake the meatballs on the center rack of the oven until they are cooked through and reach an internal temperature of 155 degrees, about 20 minutes.

Yield: 12 meatballs

Suggested wine: Chianti Classico, Agricola San Felice, Tuscany, Italy

Grilled Flank Steak with Mushroom Sauce

Flank steak marinade (recipe follows)

2 pounds whole flank steak

1 (10¾-ounce) can consommé

¾ cup dry red wine

1 celery rib, rinsed and cut into 2-inch pieces

1 carrot, rinsed, peeled and cut into 2-inch pieces

½ teaspoon rosemary

1 small yellow onion, rinsed, peeled and quartered

4 tablespoons (½ stick) butter

1 cup thickly sliced baby bell mushrooms

1 package rice pilaf

Marinate the flank steak overnight in the refrigerator.

Combine the consommé and red wine in a saucepan over medium heat. Add the celery, carrots, rosemary, and onion. Bring to a boil while stirring. Lower the heat and simmer until reduced and slightly thicker, about 45 minutes. Remove the celery, carrots, and onions with a slotted spoon and discard them.

Melt the butter in another pan. Sauté the mushrooms until soft. Stir the mushrooms and butter into the red wine sauce. Cover and keep the red wine reduction warm over low heat.

Prepare rice pilaf according to the instructions on the package.

Prepare a grill for high heat.

Grill the flank steak directly over hot coals or a gas grill set on high heat. After a few minutes, give the steak a quarter turn clockwise and continue cooking until juices form on top. Turn over the steak and repeat the quarter turn after a few minutes. To test for doneness, make a small cut halfway into the meat. Medium steak will be slightly pink in the center.

Remove the steak from the grill and let it rest 10 minutes. Slice it diagonally across the grain. Reassemble the steak over a bed of rice pilaf on a serving platter. Drizzle the red sauce over the steak and serve.

Yield: 4 to 6 servings

Suggested wine: Fleurie, Georges Duboeuf, Beaujolais, France

Flank Steak Marinade

1½ cups olive oil

¾ cup soy sauce

¼ cup Worcestershire sauce

½ cup dry red wine

⅓ cup lemon juice

2 cloves garlic, peeled and chopped

1 tablespoon dry mustard

Combine the ingredients. Put flank steak or any other cut of beef in a pan and cover with the marinade. Cover with plastic wrap and refrigerate for 24 hours.

Yield: 3½ cups

Beef Braciola

1½ pound round or top round steak, ½-inch thick

½ cup raisins

½ cup white or wild rice

¼ cup pine nuts, roasted

1 (28-ounce) can tomato sauce

2 cloves garlic, minced

¼ teaspoon dried basil

¼ teaspoon dried oregano

½ teaspoon kosher salt

½ teaspoon freshly ground pepper

½ cup sliced mushrooms

2 tablespoons grated Parmigiano-Reggiano cheese

Have the butcher run the steak through a mechanical tenderizer or pound it with a meat-tenderizing mallet on a cutting board. Cover the steak and set it aside.

Preheat the oven to 350 degrees.

Soak the raisins in ¼ cup of hot water in a small mixing bowl.

Cook the rice according to the directions on the package and set it aside to cool.

Spread the pine nuts on a baking sheet and roast them in the oven until oil comes to the surface, about 5 minutes.

Heat the tomato sauce, garlic, basil, oregano, salt, and pepper. Cover and let simmer, stirring occasionally.

Cover the meat with plastic wrap. Using the flat side of a mallet, pound the meat to a ¼-inch thickness.

Lay out the meat with the longest side facing you. Spread the cooked rice evenly over the meat. Sprinkle the mushrooms, raisins, and pine nuts in even layers over the rice.

Fold over the right and left sides of the meat to form a large rectangle. Tightly roll the meat away from you and tie it with several strands of butcher's twine. Put the meat in a roasting pan and pour half the tomato sauce over it.

Bake the braciola, basting occasionally with the sauce and pan juices, until the internal temperature reaches 160 degrees, about 50 minutes. Add water to the pan, if needed.

Remove the braciola from the oven and let it rest while the temperature rises to 165 degrees, about 10 minutes. Place it on a serving platter, ladle additional sauce over it, and dust it with grated Parmigiano-Reggiano. Serve with extra sauce and cheese on the side.

Yield: 4 to 6 servings

Suggested wine: Nebbiolo, Corino, Langhe, Italy

Ribeye Steak with Figs and Boursin Cheese

When grilling meat, remove it from the grill before it reaches the desired doneness, as the internal temperature will rise another 5 degrees off heat.

½ cup ripe figs

¾ cup balsamic vinegar

3 tablespoons cracked peppercorns

4 (½-pound) ribeye steaks, trimmed

1 teaspoon kosher salt

½ pound boursin cheese

Purée the figs and vinegar in a blender.

Put the steaks in a small baking dish and rub the cracked peppercorns into them. Dust both sides of the steaks with kosher salt. Drizzle the fig and vinegar marinade over the steaks. Cover and refrigerate for 2 hours, turning once.

Melt the boursin in a small saucepan over medium-low heat while stirring frequently. Remove the saucepan from the heat. Cover the cheese and set it aside.

Prepare coals or a gas grill to high heat. Remove the steaks from the marinade and place them on the grate directly over the heat to let them sear. After 3 minutes, use tongs to turn the steaks a quarter turn. After the steaks begin to sweat uniformly on top, flip them over. After 3 minutes, give them another quarter turn and cook to the desired doneness, following the chart below.

Serve the steaks with the melted cheese.

Yield: 4 servings

Suggested wine: Cool Climate Syrah, Cline, Sonoma, California

Steak Grilling Chart

Doneness	Internal temperature	Internal color
Rare	120°–125°	Very Red
Medium Rare	125°–135°	Some Red
Medium	135°–145°	Pink
Medium Well	145°–155°	Some Pink
Well Done	155°–165°	No Pink

Beef Tenderloin Crostini with Gorgonzola

You can also make this using premium sliced roast beef from the deli. Choose a variety that's tender, peppered on the outside, and flavored with a hint of garlic. Before you buy, ask for samples to taste and compare. To crumble Italian Gorgonzola, use a fork and mash the cheese on a paper towel.

2 pounds beef tenderloin, trimmed and tied

Kosher salt and freshly ground pepper

3 cloves garlic

½ cup pine nuts

⅔ cup Parmigiano-Reggiano cheese, grated

1 teaspoon kosher salt

½ teaspoon freshly ground pepper

3 cups fresh basil

⅔ cup extra-virgin olive oil, plus additional for serving

2 French baguettes, sliced diagonally into ½-inch pieces

½ cup crumbled Italian Gorgonzola cheese

Prepare the tenderloin a day ahead. Preheat the oven to 425 degrees.

Lightly season the tenderloin with kosher salt and pepper in a roasting pan. Roast the meat for 10 minutes. Lower the heat to 350 degrees and bake until the internal temperature reaches 125 degrees, another 10 to 15 minutes. Remove the roast from the oven and let it cool. Cover the roast and refrigerate it overnight.

The next day, preheat the oven to 375 degrees.

For the pesto, blend the garlic, pine nuts, Parmigiano-Reggiano, salt, pepper, basil, and oil in a blender or food processor until smooth.

Put the slices of baguette on a baking sheet and brush them generously with pesto. Thinly slice the beef tenderloin. Place slices of beef over the pesto. Drizzle olive oil lightly over the beef. Loosely cover the baking sheet with foil and put in the oven for 10 to 12 minutes.

Remove the crostini from the oven and sprinkle crumbled Gorgonzola cheese over them. Serve warm with extra-virgin olive oil on the side.

Yield: 4 to 6 servings

Suggested wine: Pinot Noir, Castle Rock, Mendocino, California

Osso Bucco with Porcini Mushrooms

1 ounce dried porcini mushrooms
8 medium veal shanks, crosscut 2-inches thick
Salt and freshly ground pepper
All-purpose flour
3 tablespoons unsalted butter
3 tablespoons extra-virgin olive oil
1 large carrot, chopped
2 stalks celery, chopped
1 medium onion, chopped
4 cloves garlic, chopped
2 bay leaves
1 cup dry Marsala wine
2 cups beef broth
1 cup canned Italian tomatoes with their juice
2 tablespoons finely chopped fresh parsley

Cover the mushrooms with 2 cups of lukewarm water in a small bowl and soak for 20 minutes. Strain the mushrooms and rinse them well. Coarsely chop the mushrooms.

Put the veal shanks in a shallow platter. Season them lightly with salt and pepper. Dust the surface of the veal thoroughly with flour and tap off any excess.

Heat the butter and oil in a large, heavy skillet over medium heat. When the butter foams, add the veal and cook until golden on all sides, 6 to 7 minutes. Remove the veal from the skillet and set it aside.

Cook the carrot, celery, onion, garlic, and bay leaves in the skillet on medium heat, stirring until softened, 5 to 6 minutes. Stir in the porcini mushrooms and season to taste with salt and freshly ground pepper.

Raise the heat to high and return the veal to the skillet. Add the Marsala wine and cook until the wine is almost completely reduced, 5 to 6 minutes. Add the broth and tomatoes and bring to a boil.

Lower the heat and cover the skillet. Cook until the meat is falling away from the bone, about 3 hours. Baste the meat a few times during cooking, adding more broth, if needed.

Stir in the parsley and serve piping hot.

Yield: 8 servings

Suggested wine: Mara Ripasso, Cesari, Veneto, Italy

Veal Marsala

You can also use this recipe for Chicken Marsala, substituting boneless, skinless chicken breasts for the veal.

1 pound veal cutlets, pounded thin
All-purpose flour
2 tablespoons (¼ stick) butter plus additional, if needed
1 tablespoon extra-virgin olive oil plus additional, if needed
Paprika
1½ pounds fresh white mushrooms, sliced
1 medium onion, quartered and thinly sliced
2 tablespoons chopped chives
2 tablespoons chopped Italian parsley
1 teaspoon thyme leaves
Salt and freshly ground pepper
1½ cups beef broth
¾ cup Marsala wine
1 lemon, quartered
Lemon zest

Preheat the oven to 350 degrees.

Cover the veal with waxed paper and pound it thin with the smooth side of a mallet. Dust the veal with flour.

Heat 1 tablespoon butter and 1 tablespoon olive oil in a skillet over medium-high heat. Sauté the veal until lightly browned, adding more butter and oil, if needed.

Transfer the veal to a baking dish and lightly with paprika.

Add more butter to the skillet. Sauté the mushrooms and onion over medium heat until soft, about 5 minutes. Add the chives, parsley, thyme, salt, pepper, beef broth, and Marsala. Simmer for 5 minutes.

Pour the mixture over the veal. Bake the veal, uncovered, for 30 minutes.

To serve, squeeze lemon juice over the veal and garnish with lemon zest.

Yield: 4 servings

Suggested wine: Valpolicella, Allegrini, Veneto, Italy

Pan-Seared Veal Chops with Oyster Mushrooms

6 veal rib chops, cut and trimmed ¾-inch thick, French boned
2 tablespoons (¼ stick) unsalted butter
2 tablespoons extra-virgin olive oil plus additional, if needed
Kosher salt and freshly ground pepper
1 pound fresh oyster mushrooms, rinsed

Preheat the oven to 350 degrees.

Melt the butter and oil in a large skillet over medium-high heat. Season both sides of the chops with salt and pepper. Sauté the chops until browned, 3 to 5 minutes per side.

Transfer the chops to a baking dish, cover with foil and bake the chops in the oven for 10 minutes.

Return the skillet to the heat and add the mushrooms. With a spoon, scrape the pan and stir to sauté the mushrooms until limp, about 5 minutes. If needed, add oil to keep the mushrooms from sticking.

Serve the chops smothered with mushrooms.

Yield: 4 to 6 servings

Suggested wine: Merlot, Simi Winery, Sonoma, California

Pork Chops with Creamy Mustard Sauce

1½ cups canned chicken broth

¾ cup dry white wine

½ cup golden raisins

½ cup natural (dark) raisins

2 tablespoons paprika

¼ teaspoon salt

½ teaspoon freshly ground pepper

4 pork loin chops, 1½-inches thick

¼ cup olive oil

2 medium yellow onions, chopped medium fine

4 tablespoons Dijon mustard

¾ cup heavy cream

2 tablespoons fresh cilantro, plus additional for garnish

1 lemon, thinly sliced

Preheat the oven to 350 degrees.

Bring the chicken broth, red wine, and raisins to a boil in a saucepan. Lower the heat and simmer until the raisins are plump, about 15 minutes.

Combine the paprika, salt, and pepper. Rub the chops with the mixture. Heat 1 tablespoon olive oil in a skillet. Sear the pork chops until browned on both sides.

Transfer the chops to a baking dish. Bake until the internal temperature reaches 145 degrees, 15 to 20 minutes. Remove the chops from the oven and cover them.

Meanwhile, heat the remaining 3 tablespoons olive oil in the skillet over medium-high heat. Sauté the onions and cilantro with a pinch of salt and pepper until the onions are golden brown. Stir in the hot chicken broth mixture. Add the mustard and heavy cream. Simmer until the sauce thickens.

Place the pork chops on a serving platter. Pour the mustard sauce over them and sprinkle with chopped cilantro. Serve with lemon slices on the side.

Yield: 4 servings

Suggested wine: Petite Sirah Lake County, Guenoc, Middletown, California

Panfried Pork Chops with Fresh Pear Chutney

3 tablespoons vegetable oil

1 medium onion, diced

2 garlic cloves, minced

2 tablespoons minced fresh ginger

1 cup pear vinegar

¼ cup lemon juice

¾ cup currants

1 cup light brown sugar

½ teaspoon allspice

⅛ teaspoon cayenne pepper

¼ cup lemon zest

4 Bosc pears, cored and cut into ⅜-inch cubes

6 center cut pork loin chops, 12 ounces each, trimmed

2 tablespoons olive oil

Kosher salt and freshly ground pepper

Sauté the onion, garlic, and ginger in vegetable oil in a saucepan over medium heat until the garlic is soft and begins to brown.

Add the vinegar, lemon juice, currants, brown sugar, allspice, cayenne pepper, and lemon zest. Cook and stir until the mixture begins to boil. Lower the heat and simmer until the mixture thickens.

Add the pears and simmer until they soften. Cover the chutney and set it aside.

Heat the olive oil in a large skillet over medium heat. Season both sides of the chops with salt and pepper. Fry them until golden brown, turning once. Don't overcook them—the time will vary according the thickness of the chops. The chops will be done when the internal temperature reaches 145 degrees.

To serve, spoon chutney on the plate and place a chop on the chutney. Add more chutney on top.

Yield: 6 servings

Sausage-Stuffed Pork Chops

2 slices stale dark rye bread, cut into ½-inch pieces

¼ cup chopped hazelnuts

2 tablespoons olive oil

2 links sweet Italian sausage, casing removed

½ onion, chopped

1 rib celery, chopped

¼ cup chopped parsley leaves

2 (2-inch thick) pork rib chops, bone-in

½ teaspoon paprika

½ teaspoon kosher salt

½ teaspoon freshly ground pepper

½ teaspoon rosemary

1 clove garlic, minced

Preheat the oven to 350 degrees.

Toast the bread and hazelnuts on a baking sheet until oily and lightly browned. Remove them from the oven and let cool.

To make the stuffing, heat 1 tablespoon olive oil in a large skillet over medium heat. Add the sausage, onion, and celery and cook until the onion becomes soft.

Stir in the parsley, bread, and hazelnuts. Remove the dressing from the heat and set it aside.

Butterfly the pork chops through to the rib bone, leaving the meat attached to the bone.

To make the rub, mix the paprika, salt, pepper, rosemary, and garlic in a small bowl. Rub evenly over the top and bottom of the pork chops.

Fry the chops in the remaining 1 tablespoon of oil in a large skillet until lightly browned, turning once.

Put the chops in a baking pan. Fill them with stuffing and bake until the internal temperature reaches 145 degrees, about 45 minutes.

Yield: 2 servings

Suggested wine: Zinfandel, Seghesio Family Vineyards, Healdsburg, California

Stuffed Pork Tenderloin with Apricot Sauce

3 pounds whole pork tenderloin
1 tablespoon unsalted butter
1 garlic clove, thinly sliced

STUFFING:

1 orange
1½ cups breadcrumbs
½ cup mixed, candied fruit
1 tablespoon finely chopped parsley
1 tablespoon finely chopped onion
1 garlic clove, minced
½ tablespoon chopped fresh tarragon
½ teaspoon kosher salt
1 teaspoon freshly ground pepper
4 tablespoons (¼ stick) melted unsalted butter
1 egg

SAUCE:

2 cups finely chopped dried apricots
Orange juice
1 tablespoon brown sugar
1 tablespoon lemon juice
½ teaspoon curry powder

Preheat the oven to 325 degrees.

To make the stuffing, finely grate the rind from the orange. Peel the orange and divide it into segments. Trim the skin away from the segments and cut the flesh into small pieces.

Mix the breadcrumbs, candied fruit, parsley, onion, garlic, tarragon, orange zest, orange pieces, salt, and pepper in a bowl. Stir in the melted butter. Whisk the egg lightly and add it to the stuffing to bind the mixture.

Slit the tenderloin lengthwise through half its thickness and lay open the meat. Cover it with plastic wrap or waxed paper and pound it gently with a mallet or the flat edge of a knife.

Spread the stuffing on the flattened tenderloin and roll the meat tightly into a log. Tie the rolled tenderloin with butcher's twine.

Melt 1 tablespoon butter in a roasting pan over medium heat. Sauté the sliced garlic until soft, but not brown. Add the rolled pork and sauté for a few minutes, turning often, until lightly browned on all sides.

Cover the pan with a lid or heavy foil and bake in the middle of the oven until the internal temperature reaches 145 degrees, about 45 minutes.

To prepare the sauce, put the dried apricots in a saucepan with enough orange juice to cover. Cook, uncovered, over medium heat until tender. Stir in the sugar, lemon juice, and curry powder and cook until the mixture thickens, about 5 minutes.

Before serving, remove the butcher's twine and slice the meat into 1-inch-thick pieces. Arrange the meat on a serving dish and spoon a little of the sauce over each slice. Serve the remaining sauce on the side.

Yield: 6 to 8 servings

Suggested wine: The Footbolt Shiraz, d'Arenberg, McLaren Vale, Australia

Pork Kebabs with Pine Nuts

3 pounds pork roast, trimmed

¼ cup plus 2 tablespoons olive oil

2 teaspoons freshly ground pepper

1 tablespoon kosher salt

1 tablespoon fresh rosemary

1 each green, red, and yellow bell pepper, seeded

2 medium onions

½ cup pine nuts

4 cloves fresh garlic, chopped

Preheat the oven to 300 degrees.

Cut the pork roast into 1½-inch cubes. Put the pieces in a mixing bowl. Add ¼ cup of the olive oil, the pepper, salt, and rosemary. Mix well. Cover and refrigerate for 1 hour.

Cut the peppers into 1-inch strips, then cut the strips into squares. Cut the onions in half, then quarter each half. Peel apart the onion layers.

Spread the pine nuts on a baking sheet and toast them in the oven until oily and light golden brown, 8 to 10 minutes.

Prepare a grill for high heat.

Skewer the meat and vegetables, alternating between pieces of pork, onion, and peppers. Grill the kebabs over hot coals or on a gas grill set to high.

Sauté the garlic in 2 tablespoons olive oil until it begins to soften. Remove the pan from the heat.

Remove the kebab meat and vegetables from the skewers and add them to the pan. Mix in the pine nuts and spoon onto a serving platter.

Yield: 8 to 10 servings

Suggested wine: Pinot Noir, Cloudline Cellars, McMinnville, Oregon

Classic Ham Loaf

BASTING LIQUID:

¼ cup vinegar

¼ cup water

1 teaspoon cornstarch

½ teaspoon dry mustard

½ cup packed brown sugar

HAM LOAF:

1½ pounds ground pork

1½ pounds ground ham

2 large eggs

1 cup crushed saltine crackers

1 teaspoon freshly ground pepper

4 drops Tabasco

Milk

Preheat the oven to 300 degrees.

Combine the vinegar, water, cornstarch, mustard, and brown sugar in a saucepan over medium heat. Stir occasionally until the mixture becomes clear, then lower the heat.

Mix the pork, ham, eggs, crackers, pepper, and Tabasco by hand in a bowl until the ingredients are evenly distributed. Add a small amount of milk to slightly moisten the mixture. Form into a loaf.

Put the ham loaf in a baking pan lightly greased with shortening. Bake until the internal temperature reaches 155 degrees, about 2½ hours, basting often during the final hour.

Yield: 8 to 10 servings

Suggested wine: Vin Gris of Pinot Noir, Saintsbury, Carneros, California

Baked Lamb Chops with Tomato-Olive Sauce

Salt and freshly ground pepper

6 thick lamb rib chops, French-boned

1 tablespoon extra-virgin olive oil

1 garlic clove, peeled and chopped

4 medium tomatoes, peeled and sliced

¼ cup capers

¼ cup chopped Kalamata olives

1 tablespoon all-purpose flour

Preheat the oven to 375 degrees.

Sprinkle salt and pepper on both sides of the chops.

Heat the olive oil in a skillet over medium heat. Sauté the chops with the garlic until lightly browned on both sides, 10 to 15 minutes.

Put the tomato slices, capers, and olives in a shallow casserole. Evenly sprinkle the flour, salt, and pepper over them.

Place the chops on the mixture in the casserole. Drizzle the skillet drippings over the chops.

Cover and bake until the internal temperature reaches 145 degrees, about 1 hour.

Serve on a platter, bone side up, smothered with tomatoes, olives, and capers.

Yield: 4 servings

Suggested wine: Vitiano-Cabernet/Merlot/Sangiovese-Vinicola Falesco, Umbria, Italy

Grilled Lamb Chops

8 cloves garlic, peeled and smashed

Juice of 2 lemons

¾ cup extra-virgin olive oil

1 teaspoon black peppercorns, crushed

8 lamb rib chops, French-boned

Combine the garlic, lemon juice, oil, and pepper in a blender or food processor. Transfer the mixture to a baking dish. Add the lamb chops. Cover tightly and refrigerate for 1 hour, turning once.

Prepare a grill for high heat.

Grill the chops directly over the heat, 3 to 5 minutes per side.

Yield: 4 servings

Suggested wine: Silver Label Cabernet Sauvignon, B. R. Cohn Winery, Kenwood, California

Flame-Grilled Lamb Kebabs

1 medium eggplant

2 pounds boneless leg of lamb, trimmed

1 each green, yellow, and orange bell pepper, seeded

1 Vidalia or other sweet onion

12 grape tomatoes

½ cup olive oil

1 teaspoon rosemary

¼ teaspoon allspice

2 cloves garlic, minced

Cut the eggplant into 1-inch slices and dust both sides with salt. Set aside for 10 minutes.

Cube the lamb into 1½-inch pieces. Cut the peppers into 1½-inch strips, then cut the strips into squares. Cut the onion into half, then cut each half into quarters. Peel apart the layers of onion. Skewer the pieces, alternating lamb, pepper, onion, and tomato.

Blend the olive oil, rosemary, allspice, and garlic. Brush the skewered meat and vegetables with the mixture. Dust the skewers with salt and pepper.

Prepare a grill for high heat.

Brush the eggplant with olive oil and grill it directly over the heat, turning once. To keep the eggplant warm, move it away from the heat to the outside of the grill.

Grill the skewers directly over the heat, basting with the remaining olive oil mixture.

Serve the kebabs over slices of eggplant.

Yield: 4 to 6 servings

Suggested wine: Cabernet Sauvignon, Three Rivers, Walla Walla, Washington

Stuffed Leg of Lamb

1 leg of lamb, trimmed and boned
Kosher salt and freshly ground pepper
Olive oil
1 cup chopped sun-dried tomatoes in oil
1 pound feta cheese, crumbled
4 shallots, diced
6 cloves garlic, chopped
¼ cup fresh parsley, without stems
¼ cup fresh thyme
2 tablespoons chopped fresh mint

Preheat the oven to 350 degrees.

Slice open the lamb and lay it out flat. Slice the thicker parts thinner by making horizontal cuts into, but not through, the meat, and butterfly those sections.

Dust the lamb with salt and pepper. Drizzle it with olive oil.

Spread the sun-dried tomatoes, feta, shallots, garlic, and fresh herbs evenly over the lamb.

Roll the meat across the width to form a wrap. Secure it with butcher's twine. Put the meat in a roasting pan and drizzle it with olive oil. Cover the pan loosely with foil and place it on the middle rack in the oven.

Roast until the internal temperature reaches 165 degrees, about 40 minutes.

Yield: 10 to 12 servings

Suggested wine: Cabernet Sauvignon, The Hess Collection Winery, Napa Valley, California

Grilled Leg of Lamb with Walnut Mint Pesto

1 whole leg of lamb, boneless, trimmed and butterflied open
2 batches of walnut mint pesto rub (page 202)

Open the butterflied lamb and cut it into three or four pieces of about equal size.

Put the lamb in a large baking dish. Rub pesto on all surfaces of the lamb. Reserve some pesto as a sauce for the table.

Cover the baking dish tightly with plastic wrap and refrigerate the lamb for 24 hours.

Prepare a grill for high heat.

Grill the lamb directly over the heat. After 5 to 6 minutes, rotate each piece a quarter turn. Continue to cook for an additional 5 to 6 minutes on the first side. Flip over the lamb and repeat the grilling procedure used on the first side. Test for doneness by making a small cut in the meat—it should be slightly pink.

Remove the lamb from the grill and let it rest 5 minutes before carving.

Yield: 10 to 12 servings

Suggested wine: Syrah, Qupé, Central Coast, California

Lamb Crown Roast with Wild Rice and Goat Cheese Stuffing

1½ cups packaged blend of wild, white, and brown rice

½ cup coarsely diced chorizo

4 tablespoons (¼ stick) unsalted butter

1 large onion, finely diced

1 tablespoon minced garlic

2 carrots, finely chopped

1 celery stick, chopped

¾ pound stale country bread, cubed

6 ounces goat cheese

2 tablespoons finely chopped fresh parsley

1 tablespoon finely chopped fresh thyme

1½ cups chicken stock, plus extra, if needed

1 (3-rack) lamb crown roast, French-boned, trimmed, and tied.

Preheat the oven to 450 degrees.

Cook the rice mixture according to the instructions on the package. Cover and set aside.

Cook the chorizo in a saucepan over medium heat until the fat is rendered and the chorizo is slightly crisp. Drain it on paper towels.

Melt the butter in a large saucepan over medium heat. Cook the onion, garlic, carrots, and celery until tender but not browned, about 5 minutes.

Add the rice, chorizo, bread, cheese, parsley, thyme, and stock and stir to combine. The mixture should be quite wet. Add a little more stock or water, if needed. Season to taste with salt and pepper.

Spoon the stuffing into the center of the crown roast. Wrap foil over the ends of the ribs to prevent charring. Transfer any leftover stuffing to a buttered baking dish.

Sear the roast in the oven for 10 minutes. Lower the heat to 350 degrees and put the dish with the leftover stuffing in the oven.

Continue roasting the lamb until the internal temperature reaches 145 degrees, 12 to 15 minutes per pound for medium rare. Bake any leftover stuffing, uncovered, until done, 25 to 30 minutes.

Yield: 6 to 8 servings

Suggested wine: Cabernet Sauvignon, Sterling Vineyards, Napa Valley, California

Meat Roasting Secrets
Rubs and Pestos

While marinades usually get top billing, rubs and pestos can add more interesting flavors and textures to slow-cooked meats. Before roasting, grilling, or smoking, try encrusting the meat with a rub or pesto. Here are a few of our favorites for roasts and rib cuts of beef, pork, and lamb.

All-Purpose Seasoning

For meat, poultry, potatoes, and grilled vegetables.

3½ teaspoons sweet Hungarian paprika
1 tablespoon garlic powder
1½ teaspoons onion powder
1½ teaspoons powdered oregano
1½ teaspoons powdered thyme
1 tablespoon kosher salt
1½ teaspoons freshly ground pepper
1½ teaspoons ground red pepper

Combine the ingredients in a jar or container. Cover tightly and shake vigorously until the spices are well mixed.

Yield: about ¼ cup.

The Perfect Pork Rub

For pork chops, spareribs, baby back ribs, and whole pork loin roast.

2 tablespoons finely chopped fresh thyme leaves
2 tablespoons finely chopped fresh sage
2 tablespoons fresh rosemary
4 cloves fresh garlic, finely chopped
2 tablespoons kosher salt
1 teaspoon red pepper flakes

Combine the ingredients in a small mixing bowl.
Sprinkle the rub on the meat and rub it in, coating all surfaces.
Cover the meat and refrigerate for 12 to 24 hours prior to cooking.

Yield: ½ cup

Pork Mop Sauce for Basting

Down in Dixie, these sauces are made in buckets and mopped onto whole hog sides during pig roasts. This one is a nice basting sauce for ribs on the grill or pork roast in the oven.

- 1 teaspoon kosher salt
- 1 teaspoon sugar
- 1 teaspoon grated lemon peel
- 1 teaspoon coarsely ground pepper
- 1 teaspoon paprika
- ¼ cup lemon juice
- 1 cup apple cider vinegar
- 1 cup water
- 1 tablespoon butter
- 1 tablespoon extra-virgin olive oil

Combine the ingredients in a saucepan and simmer over low heat for 20 minutes.

Yield: 2½ cups

Walnut Mint Pesto Rub for Lamb

Encrust lamb loin chops, rib chops, or lamb roast with this pesto prior to grilling or roasting.

2 cups fresh mint leaves

4 cloves fresh garlic

1 cup shelled walnuts

¼ teaspoon kosher salt

¼ teaspoon freshly ground pepper

1 cup extra-virgin olive oil

½ cup grated pecorino Romano

Chop the mint, garlic, walnuts, salt, and pepper in a blender. With the blender running, slowly add the olive oil to form a smooth paste. Stir in the cheese by hand.

Rub the pesto all over the meat. Cover and refrigerate for 12 to 24 hours prior to roasting.

Yield: 2½ cups

Prime Pesto Rub for Beef

¼ cup fresh parsley

1½ tablespoons grated lemon peel

2 tablespoons lemon juice

3 teaspoons fresh thyme

4 to 6 crushed juniper berries

3 cloves garlic, crushed and chopped

½ teaspoon freshly ground pepper

2 to 4 drops Tabasco

½ cup extra-virgin olive oil

Combine the parsley, lemon peel and juice, thyme, juniper berries, garlic, pepper, and Tabasco in a blender. With the blender running, slowly pour in the olive oil to form a smooth paste.

Rub the pesto all over the meat. Cover and refrigerate for 12 to 24 hours prior to roasting.

Yield: ¾ cup

Christmas Dinner

Baked Brie and Apples   34

Caesar Salad   81
Prosecco, Zardetto Brut, Conegliano, Italy

Lamb Crown Roast with Wild Rice and
Goat Cheese Stuffing   199
Cabernet Sauvignon, Sterling Vineyards,
Napa Valley, California

Southern Red Garnets   119

Cauliflower and Chestnuts Au Gratin   127

Butterscotch Rum Pudding   215

Desserts

I N BROWN DEER, Wisconsin, fellow retailer Larry Ehlers invited me to his store to swap recipes. "Russ," he said, "you have to taste my newest dessert creation—my Killer Brownie." There was only one problem: it came off a cake mix box. The process was very labor-intensive. Undaunted, I took the recipe back to our kitchen and began tweaking and refining the original idea, adding the signature Belgian chocolate chips and drizzle that made it our own. We became the "Home of the Original Killer Brownie." Over the years we have concocted our Peanut Butter Krazies, Blondies, Raspberry Suicides, and No Nuts About It Brownies. Our brownies have found their way all over the United States and the world, and they have been shipped all the way to the American Embassy in Rome and the United Arab Emirates.

West Point Market's Original Killer Brownies

This recipe originated on the back of a box at a time when astronauts were moon walking. As it turned out, this one small recipe for man became one giant leap for baking. We modified it to make a brownie with guts that today is known from sea to shining sea. Your brownies will probably taste a little different than the ones we're famous for. We specify only certain brands of ingredients, mix the dough in fifty-pound batches, and bake in heavy-duty commercial ovens. And then there's that West Akron water. . . . We've got to keep a few trade secrets under our belt!

¼ pound plus 5 tablespoons unsalted butter

1 (18¼-ounce) package chocolate brownie or chocolate cake mix

⅔ cup evaporated milk

1 tablespoon water

¾ cup walnut pieces

1 cup caramel ice cream topping

⅔ cup chocolate chips

Confectioner's sugar

Preheat the oven to 350 degrees.

Grease the bottom and sides of a 9 by 9-inch baking pan.

Whip ¼ pound plus 4 tablespoons of the butter with an electric mixer until light and fluffy. Blend the cake mix, evaporated milk, water, and ½ cup of the walnut pieces with the whipped butter to make a smooth, thick batter.

Spoon half the batter into the baking pan. Bake until the top appears dry and firm, 25 to 30 minutes. Meanwhile, cover the remaining batter and set it aside in the refrigerator.

Remove the pan from the oven and let it cool to room temperature.

Spread ¾ cup of the caramel topping evenly over the brownies. Sprinkle ⅓ cup of the chocolate chips evenly over the caramel. Cover the baking pan with foil and put it in the freezer until the caramel becomes firm.

Reheat the oven to 350 degrees. Remove the remaining brownie batter from the refrigerator and let it come to room temperature.

Remove the baking pan from the freezer and spoon the remaining brownie batter evenly over the caramel. Sprinkle the remaining ¼ cup of walnut pieces evenly over the batter.

Return the brownie pan to the oven and bake it until the top appears dry and firm, an additional 25 to 30 minutes. Remove the pan from the oven and let the brownies cool.

Melt the remaining ⅓ cup of chocolate chips in a saucepan. Stir in the remaining 1 tablespoon of butter until smooth. Drizzle the chocolate over the cooled brownies.

Heat the remaining ¼ cup of caramel topping in the microwave until it can be easily poured, about 20 seconds. Drizzle it over the brownies. Refrigerate for 1 hour.

Dust the brownies generously with confectioner's sugar. To serve, cut into pieces and remove from the pan.

Yield: 9 to 16 pieces

Divine Chocolate Brownies

BROWNIES:

    8 ounces Belgian 70% bittersweet chocolate

    1½ cups all-purpose flour

    1 teaspoon baking powder

    ½ teaspoon baking soda

    ½ teaspoon salt

    ¾ pound (3 sticks) unsalted butter, at room temperature

    2 large eggs

    2½ teaspoons Madagascar bourbon vanilla extract

    1½ cups packed dark brown sugar

    12 ounces semisweet Belgian chocolate chips or pieces

TOPPING:

    2 cups chopped pecans

    1 large egg

    ¼ cup Dulce de Leche or caramel topping

    2½ cups sweetened coconut

    Confectioner's sugar

Preheat the oven to 350 degrees.

Roast the pecans on a cookie sheet until oily and golden, about 10 minutes.

Melt the chocolate in a double boiler.

Sift the flour, baking powder, baking soda, and salt.

Beat the butter, eggs, and vanilla with an electric mixer. Pour in the melted chocolate and continue to beat. Add the brown sugar and beat until completely incorporated.

Lower the mixer speed and blend the flour mixture into the butter and eggs. Stir in the chocolate chips by hand, but don't overmix.

Make the topping by whisking a large egg in a mixing bowl until fluffy. Fold in the Dulche de Leche, then the coconut and pecans.

Line a 9 by 13-inch baking pan with aluminum foil. Spray the foil or grease it lightly with shortening. Pour the batter into the pan and smooth it with a spatula. Spread the topping over the batter. Bake for 30 to 35 minutes.

Using the foil ends, lift the brownies out of the pan and put them on a cutting board. Cut the brownies into small pieces and dust them lightly with confectioner's sugar.

Yield: 12 to 15 pieces

Chewy Scottish Oatmeal Cookies

For our version of oatmeal cookies, we use dried, tart cherries instead of raisins, and thick, chewy, Scottish rolled oats.

1½ cups all-purpose flour

1 teaspoon baking soda

1 teaspoon ground cinnamon

1 teaspoon freshly grated nutmeg

1½ cups Scottish porridge oats or other thick rolled oats

½ cup chopped honey roasted pecans

¼ teaspoon salt

4 tablespoons (½ stick) butter, at room temperature

1 cup packed dark brown sugar

1 large egg

½ cup applesauce

½ cup chopped dried tart cherries

2 teaspoons Madagascar bourbon vanilla extract

Preheat the oven to 350 degrees.

Combine the flour, baking soda, cinnamon, nutmeg, oats, pecans, and salt in a bowl until well mixed.

Beat the butter, brown sugar, and egg with an electric mixer until light and fluffy. Add the applesauce, cherries, and vanilla. Mix on low speed. Add the dry flour mixture and continue mixing on low speed, scraping the sides, until completely mixed.

Line a baking sheet with parchment paper. Scoop generous teaspoons of cookie dough onto the parchment paper, flattening each cookie slightly with the spoon.

Bake until soft golden brown, 10 to 15 minutes.

Yield: 12 to 14 cookies

Granola Dream Bars

¼ pound (1 stick) unsalted butter

2 cups brown sugar

1 cup all-purpose flour

3 large eggs

1½ teaspoons Madagascar bourbon vanilla extract

1 teaspoon baking powder

¾ cup light corn syrup

½ teaspoon salt

½ cup shredded coconut

2 cups honey almond crunch granola

¼ cup chopped walnuts

¼ cup oats

¼ cup Belgian chocolate chips

¼ cup Belgian chocolate, melted

Preheat the oven to 350 degrees.

Beat the butter and ½ cup of the brown sugar thoroughly with an electric mixer until smooth and creamy. Lower the mixer speed and slowly mix in the flour until just incorporated. Lightly grease a 9 by 13-inch baking pan and press out the dough evenly over the bottom. Set the pan aside.

Beat the eggs, the remaining 1 ½ cups of sugar, and the vanilla in a large mixing bowl with an electric mixer. Mix in 3 tablespoons of flour, the baking powder, corn syrup, and salt. Stir in the coconut, granola, oats, walnuts, and chocolate chips with a spoon to make a smooth batter.

Pour the batter over the dough and bake for 20 minutes.

After the bars have cooled, slowly heat the chocolate, just until it melts. Remove the chocolate from the heat. After it has cooled slightly but still is liquid, drizzle it over the bars.

Yield: 24 bars

Rice Pudding

1 tablespoon corn starch

4 cups water

2 cups white rice

3 cups milk

1½ cups sugar

¼ cup sliced almonds

1 tablespoon ground cinnamon, plus additional for garnish

Dissolve the corn starch in a small amount of water and set it aside.

Bring 4 cups water to a boil in a saucepan over high heat. Stir in the rice. When the water begins to boil again, lower the heat. Cover and cook, stirring occasionally, until the water is almost gone.

Stir the milk and sugar into the cooked rice over low heat. Let the rice simmer until it begins to bubble.

Add the corn starch and continue stirring. When the rice reaches the consistency of pudding, remove it from the heat.

Stir in the almonds and cinnamon. Spoon the pudding into small cups and dust the tops with additional cinnamon. Let the pudding cool before serving.

Yield: 16 servings

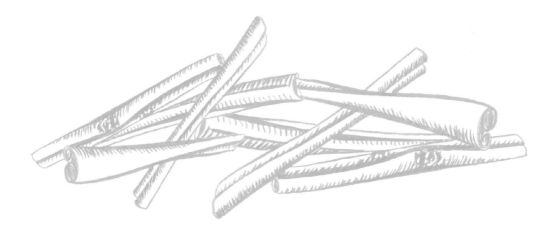

Sticky Toffee Pudding

1 cup large pitted dates

2 cups water

¾ cup all-purpose flour

½ teaspoon baking powder

½ teaspoon baking soda

6 tablespoons (¾ stick) unsalted butter, softened

2 tablespoons sugar

1 large egg

½ teaspoon Madagascar bourbon vanilla extract

½ cup heavy cream

½ cup packed light brown sugar

Preheat the oven to 350 degrees.

Bring the water to a boil in a pan over high heat. Remove the pan from the heat and stir in the dates.

Sift the flour, baking powder, and soda in a small bowl.

Using an electric mixer on medium speed, cream 4 tablespoons of the butter and the sugar until the butter becomes light. Beat in the egg and vanilla. Lower the mixer speed and add the flour mixture until just combined. Add the dates and mix for an additional 3 minutes.

Grease a large muffin tin and pour in the batter. Bake until the center is firm, about 25 minutes.

Stir together ½ cup of the cream, the light brown sugar, and the remaining 2 tablespoons butter in a saucepan over medium heat until the cream begins to boil. Continue to stir, boiling, for 5 minutes. Remove the pan from the heat and set it aside.

When the pudding is done, remove it from the oven and let it stand for about 10 minutes. While the pudding is cooling, whip the remaining ½ cup of cream. Invert the muffin tin and carefully remove the pudding.

Place each portion in a shallow serving bowl, top side down. Poke deep holes with a fork through the pudding and pour the toffee-cream sauce over it.

Serve warm with a dollop of whipped cream.

Yield: 8 servings

Chocolate Mousse

Since this is made with raw eggs, be sure to rinse them well, or use pasteurized eggs.

>   6 ounces Belgian dark bittersweet chocolate, broken into
>   ½-ounce pieces plus shavings for garnish
>   1½ cups heavy whipping cream
>   3 egg whites
>   2 tablespoons sugar

Heat 1 inch of water in the bottom of a double boiler over low heat. Put the bittersweet chocolate in the top of the double boiler. Cover and allow the chocolate to melt slowly, 9 to 10 minutes.

Remove the chocolate from the heat and stir it until smooth. Let it sit at room temperature until needed.

Chill the bowl and whisk of an electric mixer. Whisk 1½ cups heavy whipping cream on high speed until peaks form, about 1 minute.

Whisk 3 egg whites in a large stainless-steel bowl until soft peaks form, about 3 minutes. Add 2 tablespoons sugar and continue to whisk until stiff peaks form, an additional 2 to 2½ minutes.

Add a quarter of the whipped cream to the chocolate. Whisk it quickly, gently, and thoroughly. Fold the chocolate into the egg whites. Gently fold in the remaining whipped cream.

Spoon the mousse into individual glasses and refrigerate until needed.

Garnish with chocolate shavings.

Yield: 4 to 6 servings

Butterscotch Rum Pudding

4 tablespoons (½ stick) unsalted butter

1 cup dark brown sugar

1 tablespoon corn syrup

1 tablespoon dark Jamaican rum

1¾ cups milk

½ cup sugar

¾ teaspoon salt

3 tablespoons all-purpose flour

3 tablespoons cornstarch

3 egg yolks

1 teaspoon Madagascar bourbon vanilla extract

Whipped cream

Chopped walnuts

Melt the butter in a saucepan over medium heat and stir in the brown sugar, corn syrup, and rum. Continue stirring until the butterscotch reaches 250 degrees on a candy thermometer, about 15 minutes. Lower the heat and cover the saucepan.

Heat 1¼ cups of the milk, the sugar, and salt over medium heat in another saucepan. Stir until the milk just begins to boil and remove the saucepan from the heat.

Stir together the flour, cornstarch, egg yolks and the remaining ½ cup of milk in a mixing bowl until the batter is smooth. Pour the hot milk mixture into the bowl in a slow, steady stream while whisking continuously. Pour the mixture back into the saucepan and put it over low heat. Bring it to a boil, whisking continuously, until it thickens into custard.

Remove the custard from the heat and whisk in the vanilla. Combine this mixture with the hot butterscotch. Pour the combined filling into tall fluted serving glasses. Allow the glasses to cool and refrigerate them until the butterscotch sets.

To serve, fill the remainder of the glass with whipped cream and top with chopped walnuts.

Yield: 4 to 6 servings

English Trifle

Bird's Custard Powder dates back to 1837. It is the British original against which all other custards are judged. We carry both the instant variety and the traditional version that requires stovetop preparation.

1 slice pound cake, cut into ½-inch squares

¼ cup olorosos cream sherry (sweet)

7 fresh strawberries, quartered

10 fresh raspberries

1 cup Bird's Custard

2 teaspoons strawberry jam

Whipped cream

Begin layering ½-inch squares of pound cake on the bottom of a large rounded wine glass or martini glass. Pour 2 tablespoons of sherry over the pound cake. Add half of the strawberries mixed with 5 raspberries. Spoon ½ cup of custard over the berries.

Repeat with another layer of pound cake, sherry, berries, and custard.

Spoon four ½-teaspoon dollops of strawberry jam around the rim of the glass. Top with whipped cream.

Yield: 1 serving

Fresh Fruit and Lemon Parfait

1 cup whipping cream

2 tablespoons sugar

4 (8-ounce) jars lemon curd

Zest of 1 lemon

1½ cups sliced strawberries

1½ cups blueberries

1 cup raspberries

Sprigs of mint

Whip the cream at high speed with an electric mixer until stiff peaks form. Using a spoon, fold in the sugar, lemon curd, and lemon zest. Cover the bowl with plastic wrap and refrigerate for 2 hours.

Spoon a layer of the lemon mixture into the bottom of 6 parfait cups. Add alternating layers of fruit and lemon parfait until the cups are full. Serve with a sprig of mint on top.

Yield: 6 servings

Poached Pears and Cherries in Port

Pears and port are delicious with blue cheese. Complement this dish with individual Roquefort Butter Balls (page 36). Make half of the butter ball recipe, forming the mixture into six walnut-size balls. Place one on each pear's serving dish with the port wine glaze.

This recipe can be refrigerated for up to three days. Be sure to let the pears return to room temperature before serving.

6 ripe Bartlett or Comice pears

1 cup water

½ cup light brown sugar

1 stick cinnamon

2 star anise

½ cup dried tart cherries

2 cups ruby port

Peel the pears, leaving them whole with the stems intact.

Bring the water, brown sugar, cinnamon, star anise, cherries, and port and to a boil in a saucepan over medium heat. Add the pears and lower the heat. Simmer until the pears are cooked through but still firm, 15 to 20 minutes.

Remove the pears from the saucepan. Stir the liquid over medium-high heat until it reduces to a thick, syrupy glaze, an additional 10 to 15 minutes. Spoon the glaze over the pears.

Yield: 6 servings

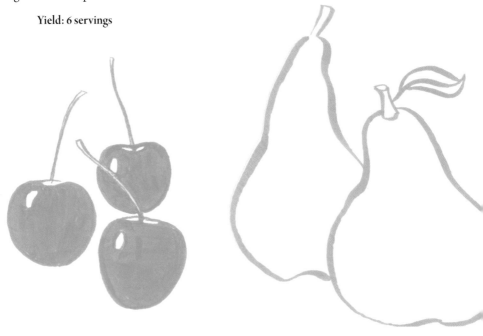

Mascarpone-Filled Pears

½ pound mascarpone cheese

4 teaspoons sugar

½ teaspoon amaretto liqueur or almond extract

2 (29-ounce) cans of pear halves, drained

1 jar raspberry preserves

1 jar chocolate raspberry dessert sauce

Confectioner's sugar

12 fresh mint leaves

Chill serving plates.

Stir the mascarpone, sugar, and amaretto in a small mixing bowl until smooth.

Match the pear halves by size. Fill the center of a pear half with a rounded scoop of mascarpone mix. Place the other pear half on top to reassemble the pear. When all the pears are assembled, cover them and refrigerate for 30 minutes.

Spread raspberry preserves on the chilled serving plates to lightly cover the bottom. Put the pears on plates and drizzle the chocolate topping over them.

Dust lightly with confectioner's sugar and garnish with fresh mint.

Yield: 12 servings

Ginger-Peach Crisp

CRUST:

>½ cup brown sugar
>
>½ cup chopped pecans
>
>2 tablespoons butter, melted

FILLING:

>3 pounds fresh peaches, peeled and sliced
>
>¼ cup dark brown sugar
>
>2 tablespoons butter, melted
>
>1 teaspoon ginger juice
>
>¼ cup minced crystallized ginger
>
>2 tablespoons lemon juice
>
>¼ teaspoon fresh grated nutmeg
>
>1 tablespoon all-purpose flour

TOPPING:

>¾ cup all-purpose flour
>
>¾ cup sugar
>
>½ cup chopped pecans
>
>6 tablespoons (¾ stick) salted butter, melted

Preheat the oven to 350 degrees.

Bring a large saucepan of water to a boil. Add the peaches and boil them for ½ minute. Cool the peaches in ice water. Remove the peach skins. Pit the peaches and slice them into wedges.

Stir together the crust ingredients in a small mixing bowl. Spread the crust mix evenly on the bottom of a 9-inch square baking dish, pressing down.

Stir together the brown sugar and melted butter in a mixing bowl. Add the ginger juice, ginger, lemon juice, nutmeg, and flour and mix the ingredients well. Toss the peaches in the mixture to coat them completely. Spoon the peach mixture into the baking dish.

Stir all the topping ingredients in a mixing bowl to create a chunky, dry mix. Sprinkle the mix evenly over the filling.

Bake until golden brown and bubbling, about 1 hour.

Yield: 9 slices

Lemony Dessert

This one is made the way mom would do it. For a fancier presentation, build this dessert high in a pie pan instead of on a rectangular baking pan. This dessert can be frozen and refrozen.

4 tablespoons (½ stick) unsalted butter, at room temperature

½ cup all-purpose flour

½ cup chopped pecans

¾ cup heavy whipping cream

½ teaspoon Madagascar bourbon vanilla extract

½ pound cream cheese

1 cup confectioner's sugar

3 cups milk

2 packages instant lemon mousse or pudding

Preheat the oven to 325 degrees.

Whip the butter with an electric mixer until smooth. Beat in the flour and pecans.

Put the mixture in a 9 by-13 inch baking pan and pat it down evenly to cover the bottom. Bake for 15 minutes. Remove it from the oven and let it cool in the pan.

Whip the heavy cream and vanilla in a bowl until stiff peaks form. In another bowl, beat the cream cheese and confectioner's sugar until smooth. Fold the cream cheese mixture into the whipped cream. Spoon it evenly over the baked crust.

Pour very cold milk into a mixing bowl. While mixing on low speed, pour in the instant mousse. Beat until the mixture thickens, 3 to 5 minutes. Pour the mixture over the whipped cream layer in the baking pan.

Cover the pan with plastic wrap and refrigerate for 2 hours.

Yield: 12 pieces

Triple Berry Mini Tarts

½ cup slivered almonds

½ cup coconut

½ cup fresh blueberries

½ cup fresh raspberries

¼ cup sliced fresh strawberries

½ cup sugar

¼ cup lemon juice

1 cup heavy whipping cream

½ pound cream cheese, at room temperature

1 (8-ounce) can of crushed pineapple, drained, with juice reserved

1 package mini tart shells

Preheat the oven to 350 degrees.

Spread the almonds on a cookie sheet and roast them in the oven for 5 minutes. Spread the coconut over the almonds and continue roasting until the nuts are oily and golden, about 5 minutes more. Be careful not to let the coconut burn.

Combine the blueberries, raspberries, strawberries, sugar, and lemon juice in a mixing bowl. Cover and refrigerate for 2 hours, stirring every 30 minutes.

Beat the heavy cream with an electric mixer until stiff peaks form. Beat the cream cheese in another mixing bowl, gradually adding ¼ cup of the reserved pineapple juice, until smooth. Fold the cream cheese mixture into the whipped cream.

Fold in the pineapple and the fruit mixture.

Fill the tart shells with the mixture. Sprinkle with almonds and coconut. Refrigerate for 2 hours before serving.

Yield: 24 tarts

Key Lime Tarts

4 shortbread cookies, crushed

¼ cup sweetened flaked coconut, toasted

2 tablespoons butter, melted

4 ounces cream cheese, softened

⅔ cup sweetened condensed milk

¼ cup key lime juice

½ teaspoon dark rum

1 package of mini tart shells

Combine the crushed cookie crumbs, coconut, and butter in a small bowl to make a coarse mixture.

Beat the cream cheese and milk with an electric mixer at medium speed until smooth. Lower the mixer speed and add the lime juice and rum.

Spoon the lime mixture into the tart shells and sprinkle with coconut topping. Put the tarts in a food container and cover them tightly. Refrigerate the tarts for several hours until set.

Yield: 12 tarts

West Point Market Pie Crust

For years we bought our pie crust dough from the best place we knew—Osman's Pies in Stow, Ohio. When that longtime family business closed, our bakers created a recipe that bakes and tastes like an Osman crust. While we don't know exactly what their recipe was, this one gets you pretty close.

2½ cups all-purpose flour
½ teaspoon salt
¼ pound (1 stick) butter, chilled
½ cup shortening, chilled
6 tablespoons water

Combine the flour and salt in a mixing bowl. Cut the butter and shortening into the flour until it reaches the texture of cornmeal.

Slowly mix in the water, just until it forms a consistent dough that isn't sticky.

Divide the dough into two balls. Flatten each ball on a floured surface to form a disk. Roll out the disks into two 11-inch circles for a 9-inch pie. Place one circle of dough in a pie pan. Trim away any dough that lies over the edge. Prick the bottom of the dough in several places with a fork to prevent air bubbles from forming during cooking.

Fill the pie shell. Place the second circle of dough over the pie pan and crimp the top and bottom shell together using your fingertips, working around the edge.

Bake at 350 degrees until light golden brown, 25 to 30 minutes.

Yield: 1 9-inch double crust

Classic Coconut Cream Pie

1 West Point Market Pie Crust (page 224)

FOR THE COCONUT FILLING:

1 pint half and half

4 egg yolks (whites reserved for meringue)

1 tablespoon of Madagascar Bourbon vanilla extract

4 tablespoons (½ stick) butter

½ cup sugar

¼ cup cornstarch

1 cup sweetened coconut flakes

FOR THE MERINGUE:

4 egg whites

½ cup sugar

Pinch of salt

Preheat the oven to 350 degrees.

Prick the bottom of the pie crust with a fork and place it into the oven. Bake it until light golden brown, 25-30 minutes. Remove the crust from the oven and set it aside to cool.

Whisk the half and half, egg yolks, and vanilla together in a small mixing bowl until slightly foamy.

Melt the butter in a saucepan over medium heat. Stir in the sugar and cornstarch. Slowly stir in the half and half mixture and let it come to a boil while continuing to stir. Stir in the coconut and remove the saucepan from the heat.

Pour the filling into the pie crust and cover it with plastic wrap. Let the filling set for 20 to 30 minutes.

Raise the oven temperature to 375 degrees.

Beat the egg whites, sugar, and salt with a mixer until stiff. Spoon the meringue on top of the coconut filling. Put the pie in the oven and brown the meringue until golden, about 5 minutes.

Remove the pie from the oven and chill it for about 30 minutes before serving.

Yield: 6 to 8 slices

Mrs. Depue's Lemon Pie

Hazel Depue was a longtime customer of the store. The first summer that her grandson Kyle worked at West Point, he entered this pie in our annual picnic and walked away with a blue ribbon for desserts, as well as Best-of-Show.

1 West Point Market Pie Crust (page 224)

2 rounded tablespoons all-purpose flour

1 cup plus 1 tablespoon sugar

3 large eggs, separated

1 teaspoon unsalted butter

Juice of 1 large lemon

1 cup cold water

Preheat the oven to 350 degrees.

Bake the pie crust until light golden brown, 25 to 30 minutes.

Whisk the flour, 1 cup of the sugar, the egg yolks, butter, lemon juice, and water in a saucepan over medium heat. Continue stirring while the mixture comes to a boil and forms a thick custard. Pour the custard into the baked pie crust.

Beat the egg whites and the remaining tablespoon of sugar with an electric mixer on high speed until the meringue holds a stiff peak.

Top the pie with the meringue and bake until brown, about 15 minutes.

Yield: 6 to 8 slices

Tropical Fruit Pie

1 cup heavy whipping cream

¼ cup sugar

⅔ cup sweetened condensed milk

1 cup crushed pineapple, drained

1 tablespoon lemon juice

½ large ripe banana, mashed

¼ cup sweetened coconut, flaked

¼ cup chopped walnuts, lightly toasted

½ cup drained and roughly chopped maraschino cherries

1 (11-ounce) can of mandarin orange wedges, drained and sectioned

1 (8 or 9-inch) graham cracker crust

Fresh mint

Whip the heavy cream with a mixer on high speed until it holds a peak. Lower the mixer speed and add the sugar.

Pour the sweetened condensed milk into the whipped cream in a steady stream while mixing with a spoon. Fold in the remaining ingredients.

Pour the batter evenly into the pie shell. Cover the shell with plastic wrap and freeze the pie for 12 hours, or until the pie is firm.

To serve, remove the pie from the freezer and let it stand for 10 minutes. Garnish with sprigs of fresh mint.

Yield: 6 to 8 slices

Key Lime Pie

CRUST:

    1½ cups crumbled gingersnap cookies

    ½ teaspoon ground ginger

    ½ teaspoon light brown sugar

    6 tablespoons (¾ stick) butter, melted

FILLING AND TOPPING:

    1 cup heavy whipping cream

    ⅓ cup plus 1 tablespoon sugar

    1 teaspoon Madagascar Bourbon vanilla

    1 teaspoon lime zest plus additional for garnish

    ½ pound cream cheese, at room temperature

    ⅓ cup lime juice

    8 ounces sour cream

Set aside 2 tablespoons of cookie crumbs to garnish the pie.

Combine the remaining crumbs, ginger, and brown sugar in a mixing bowl. Stir in the melted butter and mix well.

Pour the mixture into a 9-inch pie pan, pressing the crust mixture evenly over the bottom and up the sides of the pan. Refrigerate.

Whip the cream until stiff peaks form. Fold in ¼ cup of the sugar, the vanilla, and 1 teaspoon of the lime zest.

Beat the cream cheese and lime juice in another bowl until soft and fluffy, about 3 minutes. Fold in the whipped cream.

Spoon the filling into the pie crust. Cover and referigerate until the mixture is firm, about 4 hours.

Beat the sour cream and the remaining ¼ cup of sugar until smooth in a mixing bowl. Spread it over the pie before serving. Sprinkle with the remaining lime zest.

Yield: 6 to 8 slices

Peanut Butter Mousse Pie

CRUST:

> 2 cups coarsely chopped honey roasted pecans
>
> ¼ cup sugar
>
> 4 tablespoons (½ stick) unsalted butter, melted
>
> 1 cup Belgian semisweet chocolate chips

FILLING:

> 12 ounces cream cheese, at room temperature
>
> 1¼ cups confectioner's sugar
>
> 1½ cups smooth peanut butter
>
> ¼ cup half and half
>
> 1 tablespoon Madagascar bourbon vanilla extract
>
> 2 cups heavy whipping cream
>
> Belgian bittersweet chocolate, shaved

Preheat the oven to 350 degrees.

Thoroughly combine all the crust ingredients in a mixing bowl. Pour the mixture into a 9-inch pie pan. Pat the mixture to form an even shell on the bottom and sides of the pan.

Bake the crust for 12 minutes. Remove the pan from the oven and let it cool. Put the cooled pan in the freezer for 20 minutes.

Beat the cream cheese and ¼ cup of the confectioner's sugar with an electric mixer until smooth. Add the peanut butter and mix on low speed until it is just incorporated into the cream cheese.

Add the half and half and vanilla extract. Beat again until the mixture is fluffy.

Beat the whipping cream and 1 cup of the confectioner's sugar in another mixing bowl until soft peaks form.

Gently fold the whipped cream into the peanut butter mixture. Spoon the mix into the pie shell and cover with chocolate shavings. Cover with plastic wrap and freeze overnight.

Remove the pie from the freezer 2 hours before serving.

Yield: 6 to 8 slices

Carrot Cheesecake

½ cup raisins

2 tablespoons dark Jamaican rum

1 cup graham cracker crumbs

¼ pound (1 stick) unsalted butter, melted

3 pounds cream cheese, at room temperature

⅓ cup sour cream

¾ cup light brown sugar

3 large eggs, at room temperature

1 cup carrots, finely grated

½ cup crushed pineapple, drained

½ cup chopped walnuts

Confectioner's sugar

Preheat the oven to 350 degrees.

Put the raisins and rum in a small bowl and let soak for 20 minutes.

Combine the graham cracker crumbs and melted butter on a sheet of wax paper. Spoon the mixture into an 8-inch springform pan and pat down the crust evenly.

Beat the cream cheese in a large bowl with a mixer on high speed until light and smooth. Beat in the sour cream. Scrape down the sides of the bowl. Add the brown sugar and continue to beat. Beat in the eggs, one at a time.

Stir in the carrots, pineapple, raisins and rum, and walnuts. Pour the cheesecake mixture into the springform pan. Spread the mixture evenly.

Place the pan in a larger baking pan. Pour 1 inch of boiling water into the larger pan. Put both pans in the oven and bake for 1 hour. Turn the oven off and let the cheesecake remain in the oven for another hour.

Remove the cheesecake from the oven. After the cake is cool, remove the sides of springform pan. Cool the cheesecake in the refrigerator for 2 hours and serve, or cover it with plastic wrap and keep it overnight.

Before serving, dust the cheesecake lightly with confectioner's sugar.

Yield: 8 to 10 slices

Tiramisu Cheesecake

36 Italian ladyfingers (hard)

2 cups brewed espresso or very strong coffee

3 pounds cream cheese, at room temperature

¾ cup confectioner's sugar

3 large eggs, at room temperature

½ cup cocoa powder, sifted

½ cup heavy whipping cream

½ cup sugar

½ teaspoon Cognac, optional

Preheat the oven to 350 degrees.

Stack the ladyfingers in a large pan and pour the espresso over them. Set aside while the espresso soaks in.

Beat the cream cheese with a mixer on high speed in a large bowl until light and smooth. Beat in the sugar. Beat the eggs into the mixture, one at a time. On the lowest mixer setting, mix in the cocoa powder.

Cut out a circle of parchment paper to line the bottom of an 8-inch springform pan. Layer half of the soaked ladyfingers evenly in the bottom of the pan. Pour half of the cheesecake batter over the ladyfingers. Place the remaining ladyfingers in the pan and pour the remaining batter evenly over them.

Wrap the outside of the springform pan with foil. Place the springform pan in a larger pan. Pour boiling water 1 inch deep into the larger pan and put the pans in the oven.

Bake the cheesecake for 1 hour. Turn the oven off and leave the cheesecake in the oven for another hour. Remove the cake from the oven, remove the foil, and let the cheesecake cool. Cover the cheesecake with plastic wrap and refrigerate.

Whip the heavy cream until it forms soft peaks. Add the sugar and Cognac and whip into hard peaks. Remove the cheesecake from the pan. Top the chilled cheesecake with the whipped cream.

Yield: 8 to 10 slices

Pumpkin Cupcakes

¼ cup cream cheese

2 tablespoons unsalted butter, softened

½ tablespoon Madagascar bourbon vanilla extract

1 teaspoon orange extract

¾ cup confectioner's sugar

½ cup sugar

1 large egg

½ cup canned pumpkin

2 tablespoons chopped pecans

¼ cup vegetable oil

½ cup all-purpose flour

½ teaspoon ground cinnamon

½ teaspoon baking soda

¼ teaspoon baking powder

¼ teaspoon salt

Preheat the oven to 350 degrees. Line a muffin tin with cupcake papers.

Beat the cream cheese with a mixer on high speed in a large bowl until light and smooth. Add the butter, vanilla, and orange extract and beat until smooth. Lower the mixer speed and add the confectioner's sugar. Scrape the sides of the bowl and continue to mix the icing until light and fluffy.

Beat the sugar and egg in a mixing bowl for 2 minutes at medium speed. Beat in the pumpkin, chopped pecans, and vegetable oil.

Sift the flour, cinnamon, baking soda, baking powder, and salt over another bowl. Lower the mixer speed and add the dry ingredients. Mix to form a smooth batter.

Pour the batter into the cupcake liners. Bake the cupcakes until a toothpick inserted into the center comes out clean, 15 to 20 minutes. Let the cupcakes cool. Spread the icing over them.

Yield: 6 cupcakes

Orange Pecan Cake

1 cup freshly squeezed orange juice

3 cups sugar

½ cup all-purpose flour

2 teaspoons baking powder

Pinch of salt

2 teaspoons ground cinnamon

½ teaspoon ground nutmeg

6 large eggs, separated

¼ pound (1 stick) unsalted butter

2 cups finely chopped pecans

Zest of 1 large orange

Burnt Sugar Frosting (recipe follows)

Preheat the oven to 350 degrees.

Stir the orange juice and ¼ cup of the sugar in a saucepan over medium heat until it comes to a boil. Let boil for 3 minutes. Remove the mixture from the heat and set it aside.

Sift the flour, baking powder, salt, cinnamon, and nutmeg in a mixing bowl.

Beat the egg whites in a small mixing bowl until stiff peaks form.

Cream the butter and the remaining 2¾ cups of sugar in a large bowl with an electric mixer on medium speed until light and fluffy. Add the egg yolks, one at a time. Lower the mixer speed and add the flour mixture, scraping the sides of the bowl as needed. Fold in the pecans and orange zest. Fold the beaten egg whites into the batter until completely mixed.

Cut two 8-inch pieces of parchment paper and line the bottom of two round 8-inch cake pans. Pour the batter into the pans, spreading it evenly.

Bake until the cake is browned and a toothpick inserted into the center comes out dry, about 30 minutes.

Let the cakes cool for 20 minutes. Pierce them all over with a fork. Brush the top of the cakes liberally with the orange mixture. Let the cakes continue to cool. When they reach room temperature, cover them with plastic wrap and refrigerate overnight.

Remove the cakes from the pans. Spread Burnt Sugar Frosting evenly over one layer. Place the second layer over the first. Cover with frosting to make one 8-inch two-layer cake.

Yield: 8 to 10 slices

Burnt Sugar Frosting

3 tablespoons unsalted butter

3 cups sugar

¾ cup milk

⅛ teaspoon salt

⅓ cup boiling water

1 teaspoon Madagascar bourbon vanilla

2 tablespoons fresh orange juice

Melt the butter in a saucepan over high heat. Stir in ¾ cup of the sugar until the mixture caramelizes and becomes brown and smooth. Add the boiling water in a slow, steady stream, stirring.

Stir in the remaining sugar, milk, and salt. Continue stirring the mixture until its temperature reaches 236 degrees on a candy thermometer. If you don't have a candy thermometer, boil the mixture to the point where you can drop a small amount of it into cold water and a soft ball forms quickly.

Remove the saucepan from the heat and let the icing cool to room temperature. Add the vanilla and orange juice and whisk the frosting until it thickens.

German Chocolate Cherry Cake

CAKE:

    1 box German chocolate cake mix

    2 large eggs

    1 (20-ounce) can cherry pie filling

    1 teaspoon almond extract

DARK FUDGE FROSTING:

    5 tablespoons unsalted butter

    ⅓ cup milk

    1 cup sugar

    ½ pound Belgian bittersweet chocolate chips

Preheat the oven to 350 degrees.

For the cake, whisk 2 large eggs in a large mixing bowl until foamy. Stir in the cherry pie filling and almond extract until well mixed. Slowly add the cake mix, stirring, until thoroughly blended.

Grease a 9 by 13-inch baking pan lightly with shortening. Spoon in the cake batter.

Bake for 35 minutes.

For the frosting, melt the butter in a saucepan over medium-high heat. Stir in the milk and sugar. Bring to a boil, stirring until the sugar is completely dissolved. Remove the frosting from the heat. Add the chocolate chips, stirring until they are melted.

Frost the cake while the frosting is still warm.

Yield: 12 slices

Almond Pound Cake

1½ cups cake flour

1 teaspoon baking powder

½ teaspoon salt

⅜ pound (1½ sticks) unsalted butter, at room temperature

¾ cup sugar

1 tablespoon almond extract

2 teaspoons Madagascar bourbon vanilla extract

½ cup sour cream

3 large eggs

½ cup amaretto liqueur

Whipped cream

Fresh berries in season

Preheat the oven to 350 degrees.

Sift the cake flour, baking powder, and salt in a mixing bowl.

Cream the butter, sugar, and almond and vanilla extracts with an electric mixer until light and fluffy. Lower the mixer speed and add the eggs, one at a time, until well blended.

Add half the dry ingredients to the butter and egg mixture and continue blending at low speed until just fully incorporated.

Scrape the sides of the bowl well and add the sour cream and the remaining dry ingredients. Continue blending at low speed until the mixture is smooth and creamy.

Grease and flour a 4½ by 8½-inch pan with shortening or butter. Pour in the batter. Bake until firm and golden brown, 45 to 50 minutes.

When the cake has cooled, remove it from the pan and cut it horizontally with a serrated knife into 3 even layers. With a pastry brush, spread the Amaretto liqueur over each layer.

Place a layer on a serving tray and frost it generously with whipped cream. Distribute the berries evenly over the whipped cream. Repeat with the other two layers to make a three-layer cake.

Yield: 8 slices

Tipsy Orange Pound Cake

2½ cups sugar

¾ cup freshly squeezed orange juice

4 teaspoons grated orange zest

¼ cup of Grand Marnier or orange liqueur

3 cups all-purpose flour

½ teaspoon baking soda

½ teaspoon baking powder

1 teaspoon salt

¼ cup freshly squeezed orange juice

¾ cup buttermilk

½ teaspoon Madagascar bourbon vanilla extract

1 teaspoon orange extract

½ pound (2 sticks) unsalted butter, at room temperature

4 extra large eggs, at room temperature

12 ounces Belgian semisweet chocolate chips

Confectioner's sugar

Combine ½ cup of the sugar, ½ cup of the orange juice, the orange zest, and Grand Marnier in a small saucepan over medium heat. Whisk until the sugar is completely dissolved. Remove the saucepan from the heat, cover, and set it aside.

Preheat the oven to 350 degrees.

Sift the flour, baking soda, baking powder, and salt.

Whisk the remaing ¼ cup of orange juice, the buttermilk, vanilla, and orange extract in another bowl.

Cream the butter and sugar with an electric mixer until light and fluffy. Lower the mixer speed and add the eggs, one at a time, until well blended.

With the mixer on low, add half the buttermilk mixture to the creamed butter and eggs. Add half the flour mixture and blend until just incorporated. Add the remaining buttermilk mixture and the remaining flour and mix just until a smooth batter is formed.

Scrape down the bowl. Stir the chocolate chips into the batter. Do not overmix.

Grease and flour a 12-inch Bundt pan. Pour in the batter.

Bake until firm and golden brown, about 45 minutes. Let cool for 10 minutes.

Invert the cake onto a cooling rack and remove the pan. Place the cooling rack over a baking sheet. Poke the cake with a skewer several times through the top and sides. Brush the cake generously with the orange liqueur mixture. Let the cake dry uncovered at room temperature for one hour.

Just before serving, dust the cake with confectioner's sugar.

Yield: 6 to 8 slices

Espresso Nut Roll

FILLING:

½ cup sugar

3 tablespoons all-purpose flour

2 teaspoons instant Espresso

¼ teaspoon salt

1¼ cups of milk

1 ounce of bittersweet Belgian chocolate

1 large egg, beaten

1 tablespoon butter

1 teaspoon Madagascar bourbon vanilla

NUT ROLL:

4 large eggs, separated

½ cup sugar

1 teaspoon Madagascar bourbon vanilla

⅓ cup all-purpose flour

½ teaspoon salt

1 teaspoon baking powder

⅓ cup chopped walnuts

Confectioner's sugar

Bittersweet chocolate, shaved

Raspberry syrup

Mix the sugar, flour, instant Espresso, and salt in a saucepan. Stir in the milk and chocolate.

Cook the mixture over medium heat, stirring while it thickens.

Add the egg and continue to stir and cook until the mixture just begins to boil. Remove it from the heat and stir in the butter and vanilla. Cover the saucepan and let cool.

Preheat the oven to 375 degrees.

Beat 4 egg whites with an electric mixer until stiff peaks form. Stir in the sugar.

Beat the egg yolks and vanilla in another bowl until they thicken. Fold the yolks into the egg whites.

Sift the flour, salt, and baking powder in another bowl. With the mixer on low, add the flour to the egg mixture. Stir in the nuts.

Lightly grease a shallow 10 by 15-inch baking pan with shortening and pour in the batter. Bake for 12 minutes.

Remove the pan from the oven and let it cool slightly. When the pan is no longer hot, remove the cake by loosening the sides and inverting the pan over waxed paper that has been dusted with confectioner's sugar. Roll the cake and the waxed paper into a tight log, starting from the 10-inch end. Set it aside to cool.

Unroll the cake and spread the espresso filling evenly over the surface. Roll the cake back up without the waxed paper and refrigerate it.

Before serving, dust the cake with confectioner's sugar, spread shaved chocolate over the top, and drizzle it with raspberry syrup.

Yield: 10 slices

Ring-Rum Pound Cake

3 cups cake flour

1½ teaspoons baking powder

⅛ teaspoon salt

¼ teaspoon mace

½ pound (2 sticks) butter, at room temperature

1 teaspoon Madagascar bourbon vanilla extract

1½ cups sugar

3 large eggs

¼ cup milk

¼ cup dark Jamaican rum

Confectioner's sugar

Preheat the oven to 325 degrees.

Sift the flour, baking powder, salt, and mace three times into a mixing bowl.

Beat the butter, vanilla, and sugar with an electric mixer until smooth. Add the eggs and continue beating until the mixture is light and fluffy.

Lower the mixer speed and mix in the flour, milk, and rum.

Grease a 3-quart ring mold or Bundt pan. Pour in the batter. Bake in the oven for 60 to 65 minutes.

Remove the pan from the oven and let it cool on a rack for 1 hour. Dust a serving plate with confectioner's sugar. Invert the pan and remove the cake. Place the cake on the serving plate and dust it with confectioner's sugar.

Yield: 6 to 8 slices

Raspberry Rhubarb Sorbet

Once a quintessential summertime ingredient, rhubarb just doesn't seem to get used much any more. Although it's a vegetable (it's tart!), our favorite way to use rhubarb is as a fruit, with plenty of sugar. You'll need an electric ice cream maker or, if you want to be really authentic, freeze it in a hand-crank model with ice and rock salt. If you grow your own rhubarb, be sure to only use the stalks; discard the leaves.

1¼ cups sugar

1½ cups plus 1 tablespoon water

½ pint raspberries, rinsed

3 cups sliced fresh rhubarb stalks

2 tablespoons Grand Marnier or Cointreau

1 tablespoon lemon juice

¼ cup heavy whipping cream

Combine 1 tablespoon of the sugar, 1 tablespoon of the water, and the raspberries in a mixing bowl. Cover and refrigerate.

Bring the remaining sugar and ½ cup of the water to a boil in a saucepan over medium heat, stirring until the sugar is completely dissolved. Lower the heat and add the rhubarb. Let the rhubarb simmer for 30 minutes, stirring occasionally, until it breaks down almost to the consistency of a purée.

Pour the rhubarb and its syrup, the liqueur, lemon juice, and whipping cream into a blender or food processor and blend until smooth. Stir in the remaining 1 cup of water. Use a spoon to stir in raspberries.

Pour the mixture into an ice cream maker and process it according to the manufacturer's instructions.

Yield: 4 to 6 servings

Aztec Hot Chocolate

The delicious taste of this recipe comes from its exotic ingredients: cinnamon sticks, star anise, whole vanilla beans, and rosewater. If you can't find rosewater—West Point Market may be the only store in Ohio that carries it—make your own. For ½ cup of rose water, put ½ cup of fresh rose petals in a saucepan and add 1 cup of water. Simmer the water until reduced by half. Strain the water into a clean container and discard the petals. Cover tightly and store in the refrigerator.

> 2 cups milk
>
> ¼ piece star anise
>
> ¼ stick cinnamon
>
> 1 teaspoon rose water
>
> ¼ vanilla bean, split down the center
>
> 3½ ounces (1 bar) Valrhona 71% chocolate or any premium quality bittersweet chocolate
>
> Whipped cream

Heat the milk, star anise, cinnamon, rose water, and vanilla bean in a saucepan over medium-high heat. Bring the mixture to just under a boil, stirring often, then lower the heat.

Add the chocolate and stir until fully melted. Cover and let steep over low heat for ½ hour, stirring occasionally.

Remove the anise, cinnamon stick, and vanilla bean. Pour into 4 mugs and top generously with whipped cream.

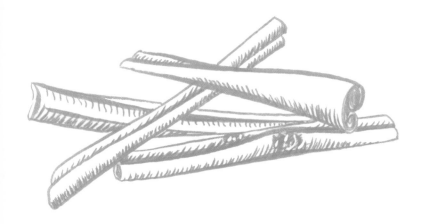

Spring Fling

Grilled Shrimp and Asparagus Salad   80
Sauvignon Blanc, St. Supéry, Napa Valley, California

Grilled Leg of Lamb with Walnut Mint Pesto   198
Syrah, Qupé, Central Coast, California

Roasted Fingerling Potatoes   118

Steamed Broccoli with Lemon and Butter

Poached Pears and Cherries in Port   218

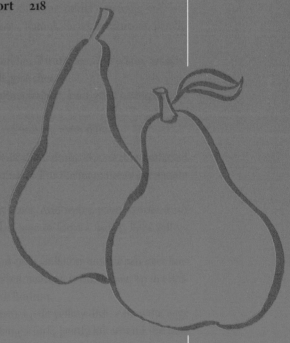

Afterword

For over seventy years West Point Market has been serving Akron and north-eastern Ohio with immense pride. We have always strived to bring our loyal customers the best quality products, but most importantly to be more than just a grocery store. I hope you have enjoyed discovering the many different recipes in this book as much as I have enjoyed sharing them with you. It has been the great joy of my life to find the best products from all over the world and bring them to the customers in our community. I look forward to continuing what I hope is a long tradition of passion for quality that has kept our business thriving for all these years.

It's been a pleasure serving you.

All the best,
Russ Vernon

Acknowledgments

Our cookbook was compiled by a number of passionate West Point Market associates who volunteered their skills, knowledge, and favorite recipes. We met regularly in the West Point kitchen, over a period of months, for afternoon tastings and feedback. With access to all the phenomenal ingredients in the store, the Cookbook Committee prepared, modified, and enhanced the recipes that are collected in this book. I am blessed, pleased, fortunate, and privileged to have been a small part of this group of foodies, and I am thankful for their passion.

Thank you to our Cookbook Committee: Flora Budo, Jessica Carlson, Pam Cartwright, Don Dillon, Elizabeth Finnegan, Dom Gionti, Apryle Griffith, David Hanna, Diane Hawk, Diana Hazlett, Kyle Klever, Norm Ross, and Larry Uhl.

Additional thanks go to Jamie Boyd and Linda Fletcher for their wine-pairing suggestions and notes, and to Tom Loraditch for menu suggestions.

It may be hard to imagine for a food store like ours, but this is the first cookbook we have ever published in the seventy-plus years that we have been in business. The University of Akron Press encouraged us to do this project in 1999 and has guided us step-by-step for over nine years. Thank you to Amy Freels, Julie Gammon, Elton Glaser, Thea Ledendecker, Mike Sees, and Carol Slatter for the editing, marketing, and project coordination, and to Anne Kachergis for the book's beautiful design. Thank you to David Giffels for the book's introduction. Thanks also to Joe Benes for the photograph of the cover illustration. A special note of thanks to Andrew Borowiec at the Press for his vision and patience in guiding this book to completion.

Finally, thank you to Doug Spence, our long-time graphic and sign illustrator, for his fabulous chalkboard drawing for the cookbook's cover and for the additional illustrations inside.

Index

Series on Ohio History and Culture

George W. Knepper, *Summit's Glory*

Leonard Sweet, *Strong in the Broken Places*

John H. White and Robert J. White Sr., *The Island Queen*

H. Roger Grant, *Ohio's Railway Age in Postcards*

Frances McGovern, *Written on the Hills: The Making of the Akron Landscape*

Keith McClellan, *The Sunday Game: At the Dawn of Professional Football*

Steve Love and David Giffels, *Wheels of Fortune: The Story of Rubber in Akron*

Alfred Winslow Jones and Daniel Nelson, *Life, Liberty, and Property:A Story of Conflict and a Measurement of Conflicting Rights*

David Brendan Hopes, *A Childhood in the Milky Way: Becoming a Poet in Ohio*

John Keim, *Legends by the Lake: The Cleveland Browns at Municipal Stadium*

Richard B. Schwartz, *The Biggest City in America: A Fifties Boyhood in Ohio*

Thomas A. Rumer, *Unearthing the Land: The Story of Ohio's Scioto Marsh*

Steve Love, Ian Adams, and Barney Taxel, *Stan Hywet Hall & Gardens*

William F. Romain, *Mysteries of the Hopewell: Astronomers, Geometers, and Magicians of the Eastern Woodlands*

Dale Topping, edited by Eric Brothers, *When Giants Roamed the Sky: Karl Arnstein and the Rise of Airships from Zeppelin to Goodyear*

Millard F. Rogers Jr., *Rich in Good Works: Mary M. Emery of Cincinnati*

Frances McGovern, *Fun, Cheap, & Easy: My Life in Ohio Politics, 1949–1964*

Larry L. Nelson, editor, *A History of Jonathan Alder: His Captivity and Life with the Indians*

Bruce M. Meyer, *The Once and Future Union: The Rise and Fall of the United Rubber Workers, 1935–1995*

Steve Love and Ian Adams, *The Holden Arboretum*